W9-AOA-205

LIFE NATURE LIBRARY

THE
FISHES

LIFE NATURE LIBRARY

THE
FISHES

by F. D. Ommanney
and the Editors of
TIME-LIFE BOOKS

TIME-LIFE BOOKS   NEW YORK

About the Author

Francis Downes Ommanney, known both in this country and in his native England for his writings on voyages to the world's out-of-the-way places, has had a long career in fisheries research and management. Following three years of lecturing on zoology at London University, he joined the staff of Britain's *Discovery* investigations in 1929, carrying out research into Antarctic whaling aboard the vessel *Discovery II*. War interrupted this work, and after six years in the Royal Navy, Ommanney joined the British colonial service in 1947, continuing his fisheries research work in Zanzibar, Singapore and Hong Kong. His books include *South Latitude*, which won the *Sunday Times* Gold Medal for "best travel book of the year" in 1938 and was published in the U.S. as *Below The Roaring Forties*, as well as numerous other travel books, *The Ocean*, published in 1949, and *A Draught of Fishes*, published in 1966.

ON THE COVER: Small barracuda speed through Pacific waters off the Marshall Islands.

Contents

TIME-LIFE BOOKS

EDITOR
Jerry Korn
EXECUTIVE EDITOR
A.B.C. Whipple
PLANNING
Oliver E. Allen
TEXT DIRECTOR   ART DIRECTOR
Martin Mann   Sheldon Cotler
CHIEF OF RESEARCH
Beatrice T. Dobie
PICTURE EDITOR
Robert G. Mason
Assistant Text Directors:
Ogden Tanner, Diana Hirsh
Assistant Art Director: Arnold C. Holeywell
Assistant Chief of Research: Martha T. Goolrick
Assistant Picture Editor: Melvin L. Scott

PUBLISHER
Joan D. Manley
General Manager: John D. McSweeney
Business Manager: John Steven Maxwell
Sales Director: Carl G. Jaeger
Promotion Director: Beatrice K. Tolleris
Public Relations Director: Nicholas Benton

LIFE NATURE LIBRARY

EDITOR: Maitland A. Edey
Associate Editor: Percy Knauth
Assistant to the Editor: John Paul Porter
Designer: Paul Jensen
Staff Writers: David Bergamini, Dale Brown,
Robert McClung, Peter Meyerson
Chief Researcher: Martha T. Goolrick
Researchers: Doris Bry, Peggy Bushong, Joan Chasin,
Mollie Cooper, Eleanor Feltser, Le Clair G. Lambert,
Paula Norworth, Victor H. Waldrop,
Paul W. Schwartz, Phyllis M. Williamson, Sybil Wong

EDITORIAL PRODUCTION
Production Editor: Douglas B. Graham
Quality Director: Robert L. Young
Assistant: James J. Cox
Copy Staff: Rosalind Stubenberg, Suzanne Seixas,
Florence Keith
Picture Department: Dolores A. Littles,
Joan T. Lynch
Art Assistants: James D. Smith, Mark A. Binn,
James K. Davis

The text for the chapters of this book was written by F. D. Ommanney, the picture essays by the editorial staff. The following individuals and departments of Time Inc. were helpful in producing the book: LIFE staff photographers Larry Burrows, John Dominis, Eliot Elisofon, Fritz Goro and Leonard McCombe; Editorial Production, Robert W. Boyd Jr., Margaret T. Fischer; Editorial Reference, Peter Draz; Picture Collection, Doris O'Neil; Photographic Laboratory, George Karas; TIME-LIFE News Service, Murray J. Gart. Reprints: Paula Arno (editor), Valentin Chu (assistant editor).

Introduction

Not only are fishes the subject of ever-expanding research by ichthyologists but they also incite the interest and whet the imagination of students and the general public, for whom a fascinating glimpse into the extraordinary world of fishes is provided by this fact-filled and beautifully illustrated volume.

Long regarded as constituting only one of the five recognized classes of back-boned animals—along with amphibians, reptiles, birds and mammals—fishes are now generally considered as making up a huge and complex group of their own comparable to all the other classes of vertebrates put together. This group, known by the Latin word *Pisces*, comprises in simplest terms the finned, gill-breathing, aquatic vertebrates, in contrast to the four-footed, lung-breathing, terrestrial vertebrates, the Tetrapoda.

Fishes outdo the tetrapods in many ways. They are immensely older in evolutionary sequence and are ancestral to all land vertebrates. Nevertheless, they are fully as diversified as the other vertebrates in structure, size, appearance, life ways and physiology. Despite hundreds of millions of years of greater antiquity, they exhibit little evidence of racial senescence; the bony fishes in particular are at the height of their evolution. Fishes today greatly surpass all land vertebrates in numbers of known species, and previously unknown kinds are constantly being discovered.

Fishes live in a fantastic variety of habitats, from lightless oceanic abysses, where pressures amount to thousands of pounds per square inch, to the boundless surface of the open sea. Inhabited also are various mid-depths of the sea, where no shore, no bottom and no surface is ever encountered, and the only light is that produced by themselves and by other luminous animals. They are found from the high tropics to the polar regions, among wave-churned intertidal rocks and coral reefs rich in life almost beyond imagining, along sandy beaches, in muddy bays, brackish estuaries, great rivers and tiny brooks, stagnant pools and rushing torrents, even in stygian caves where blind and colorless fishes live as deep as a thousand feet underground. Some fishes spend part of their existence out of the water and will drown if kept submerged; some live in a state of partially suspended animation in mud cocoons when their pools dry up, others then travel overland to new aquatic homes.

Wherever they live—and they occur with few exceptions wherever there is water—fishes have become beautifully adapted through natural selection to meet the stresses of the physical, chemical and biotic environment of which they are an integral part. Little wonder, indeed, that they are so many and so diverse.

Fishes excel also as a source of sport and recreation: anglers far outnumber hunters. And fishes provide by far the greatest wildlife crop, offering one of the major hopes of forestalling the time when the ominously expanding human population, even in the most favored lands, will run short of animal protein.

Carl L. Hubbs
Professor of Biology Emeritus
Scripps Institution of Oceanography
University of California, San Diego

1

Inheritors
of an
Ancient World

SWIMMING, wriggling, crawling, floating in the waters that cover about 75 per cent of our world is an immense population of animals whose full extent we scarcely realize. Fishes swarm this planet in millions upon millions, breeding, growing, living, dying in everything from puddles and ponds to the great oceans. There are many more species of insects, but not even the insects can match the fishes' diversity in size and shape, ranging from tiny animals to monsters 50 feet long. And of all the earth's vertebrate creatures, they are the oldest, having populated the water ages before the first of them ventured out of it onto the land to begin the long, slow evolutionary process that gave rise to the mammals and finally to man.

Yet of the lives of fishes, how they developed, how they are organized in their watery environments, we have known quite little until comparatively recent times. For the environment in which they live is to us entirely alien, and though they are in a sense our cousins, even if very distant ones, their way of life and shape long ago took a course quite different from our own. Their evolution and existence have always been conditioned by water, and water has drastically different properties from the air we know.

Exploiting every nook and niche of their vast domain, fishes have developed not only in unimaginable numbers but also in a bewildering and bizarre variety. There are archaic fishes that go back in a direct line through hundreds of millions of years of evolution—such fishes as the sharks and rays, the lampreys, the hagfishes, the lungfishes, the bichirs of Africa and the Mississippi paddlefish. There are fishes that breathe air as well as water, others that walk or fly as well as swim. There are fishes that bear live young, and others that lay eggs. There are round fishes, flat fishes, tube-shaped fishes; there are fishes which cannot lead an independent existence of their own; there are fishes that migrate thousands of miles and others that spend their entire lives in the same hole. There are at least 20,000 species of fish that we recognize—and perhaps more of whose existence we have no knowledge at all.

For all of this enormous diversity, however, there are certain characteristics common to all fishes, imposed upon them by the conditions of the medium in which they live. Above all else, their lives are shaped by the incompressibility of water, a cardinal fact dominating everything that lives or moves in it.

WATER has imposed upon fishes their general shape, their way of breathing, their method of locomotion, of feeding, of reproducing their own kind and has even given them, as we shall see, a unique sixth sense possessed by no other animal. The nature of the world of water—its shoals and depths, its temperatures and currents, the animal and vegetable life that exists in it—has offered fishes all kinds of opportunities for specialization which they have exploited fully. Life in the water has imposed upon them their basic coloration, and in its darkest depths, where no light ever penetrates, some fishes have even developed their own lighting systems while others have abandoned sight entirely and have become blind.

Almost without exception, fishes are to be found wherever there is permanent water, from mountain streams to the depths of the oceans and even in rivers underground. Few natural bodies of water are too hot, too cold or too salty to support fishes. There are even some fishes which have adapted themselves to living in pools that appear only intermittently or seasonally.

But all their various habitats have their effects on the fishes. Many of the numberless variations in structure, form, fins and the like which fishes show are simply modifications which the fish has developed to cope with a particular environment. A swift stream and a slow river present different problems in terms of currents; a shallow and a deep lake have radically different seasonal

SHAPED FOR SAFETY

The bottom-dwelling sole, flat as a plate, is rendered inconspicuous by its mottled coloration. By day it buries itself in the sandy sea floor and remains still. At night it prowls in search of worms or shrimps. The reef-dwelling butterflyfish has dual protection: a body camouflaged by bright colors with a distinctive "eye" spot to deceive predators, and a row of spines on its back that make it an unpleasant mouthful.

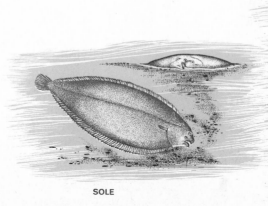

SOLE

BUTTERFLY FISH

patterns of temperature change. The ocean depths present still other possibilities for specialization—seemingly similar environments in different parts of the world may actually vary radically in the chemical nature of the water, the type of bottom, the changing seasons. In all of these conditions fishes adapt themselves, in some cases with considerable ingenuity, in such ways as to get the most benefit out of the environment in which they live.

ONCE they are established in their environment, however, few fishes will venture out of it into another, different one. Catfish hug the bottom, flyingfish are found near the surface, tropical barracudas live among the coral reefs, tuna range the open seas. Generally speaking, closely related fishes tend to occupy the same part of their environment; but there are, of course, always exceptions. In these cases, one may find, within the same family, structural adaptations and specializations as wide-ranging and as diverse in their application as those to be found in the fish population at large.

A classic example of such diversity within the family is the popular group of aquarium fishes belonging to the South American Characidae. The characins, as they are popularly known, are not an old family of fishes as fishes go, and yet in a comparatively few million years their different species have achieved a surprising variety in shape and feeding behavior. Some are long, slender and pikelike with no unusual development of the fins; others are markedly flattened with broadly expanded anal and dorsal fins; some are deep-chested fishes with large pectoral fins that enable them to fly across the surface for short distances. The bloodthirsty piranha is a member of this family, but others are specialized to feed on insects, still others off the bottom, and there are even a few that seem to be strictly vegetarian.

Yet for all this diversity, the characins are all very closely related and spring from common ancestral bonds. Like Darwin's finches, which were trapped on the Galápagos Islands and over a somewhat shorter period of time had developed many different varieties, the characins have simply adapted themselves very successfully to the many opportunities afforded them in their environment.

Habitat plays its part not only in determining a fish's shape and structure, but its color too. With few exceptions, fishes are colored according to a basic general plan—dark above and light below. But different kinds of fish have different colors according to where they live in the water. Thus those that live close to the surface tend to have a bluish or greenish cast; those that live near or on the bottom are usually brown on back and sides, while those that live in

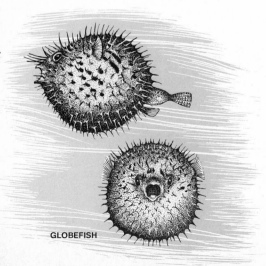

GLOBEFISH

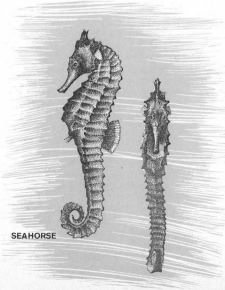

SEAHORSE

The shallows-dwelling globefish, when threatened, has the ability to quickly swallow a quantity of water to swell itself up so that predators cannot swallow it. When inflated, it is as palatable as a pincushion. The delicate, weed-dwelling seahorse is ringed with bony plates which break up its contours and help camouflage it. It gets around in the aquatic vegetation of its home by undulating its little back fin.

the abyssal depths of the sea beyond the zone of light tend to be black or silvery.

When it comes to form and structure, however, it is feeding behavior which determines the most obvious specializations and modifications among fishes. More time and energy is spent in feeding than on anything else, and according to the nature of their food, fishes develop suitable teeth and other feeding mechanisms of ingenious and varied form.

Like other animals, fishes eat a wide variety of food, alive or dead, plant or animal. Some are herbivores and eat only plants, many are carnivores, or flesh eaters; then there are primary carnivores, which feed on the herbivores, and hypercarnivores, which eat the carnivores. There are scavengers that eat only dead matter, and a good many fishes that are omnivorous, eating both plant and animal foods. A large number are plankton feeders, straining quantities of water through mouth and gill rakers to obtain the smaller organisms that drift about in the surface layers. Finally, there are fishes that suck the body fluids of other fishes.

T HE varieties of food available are seemingly endless, but it may be said, in a very general way, that fishes are characteristically carnivorous. The herbivores are few—among them are the common carp, some minnows and the parrotfish species. The latter are highly specialized, with a pronounced beaklike modification of the teeth at the front of the jaw with which they bite off pieces of plants, as well as teeth grouped farther back in the pharynx in such a way as to give the throat a paved surface against which food is ground into tiny pieces. But while this remarkable dental array is particularly suitable to eating plants, some species of parrotfish use it to good advantage in eating other forms of food as well, nipping off and crushing coral animals and occasional mollusks.

The fact that there are so relatively few plant eaters among the fishes is of considerable significance to man in his attempts to ensure a continuous and plentiful supply of food from the waters of the earth, particularly the sea. A large population of plant-eating fish might conceivably make it possible for man to replenish that population as he consumes it by resowing the plants on which the fish feed, much as he resows his pastureland for cattle, sheep and other milk- or meat-producing animals. Plants are the most efficient converters of the light energy from the sun on which all life on earth depends; yet even plants are only about 3 per cent efficient in utilizing the available light energy. The animals that eat plants have a similarly low-level conversion efficiency, and farther along the food chain the percentage steadily declines: animals that eat animals that eat plants clearly are more expensive in terms of light energy than animals that just eat plants. Thus there is as yet little hope that man can ensure fish-production levels in the oceans comparable to the food produced on land.

Yet the oceans do produce one crop in extraordinary abundance on which probably more fishes feed than any other. This is the plankton, the primeval food of the sea. It consists of myriads of both plants—phytoplankton—and animals—zooplankton—many of them single-celled and microscopic in size, drifting about the water in clouds. It has been calculated that over an entire year the net yield of plant plankton in an area such as the North Atlantic is about one ton per acre (the average yield of hay in a fertile field is a little more than one and a half tons). Nonetheless, the total amount of living plants produced annually by all the world's oceans exceeds that produced on land since, after all, the oceans constitute such a large proportion of the earth's surface. It has been estimated that the annual net production of phytoplankton amounts to nearly

WATER BALANCE IN FISHES

Since the liquids in a fresh-water fish's body are saltier than the surrounding water, it is in constant danger of soaking up water and swelling, just as a bladder of salt water in a beaker of fresh will in a laboratory experiment (above). As a result, it doesn't drink, and what water comes in through the skin and gills (dark arrows) is carried to the kidneys and used to carry away waste products in large quantities of urine (light arrow).

A salt-water fish (below) has exactly the opposite problem: its liquids are less salty than the surrounding water, and it is in constant danger of dehydration, like a shrinking bladder of fresh water in a laboratory beaker of salt water. Thus the fish must drink large quantities of water to make up for what it loses through its gills and skin. Some of the salt that it gets goes through the digestive tract and is excreted. Some is literally forced through special gill cells back into the ocean. A salt-water fish seldom urinates.

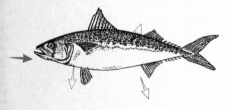

500 billion tons. Much of this production is eaten by zooplankton, and the plankton-feeding fishes in turn eat the zooplankton along with the phytoplankton. Since the plankton drifts about the oceans on or near the surface, these fishes are for the most part pelagic, or surface dwellers. Characteristically, they travel in large schools. They include such species as the herring, mackerel, menhaden, anchoveta, capelin and many others. There are nonschooling fishes among them too, one of the most notable being the largest of all living fishes, the whale shark, which grows up to 50 feet long. Among river fishes the Mississippi paddlefish is a plankton feeder.

To strain plankton from water, fishes need a sieve of some sort, and this they have developed in the form of close-set structures called gill rakers. These are attached to the gill arches opposite the gills, and are simple or branched toothlike processes arranged in rows as in a comb. Their spacing and structure determine the general size and type of the plankton retained, much as the size of the mesh in a net determines the size of the fish to be caught in it. Most of the plankton feeders obtain their food by swimming along with their mouths open and the gill covers expanded, straining quantities of water through them. The plankton collects on the gill rakers, the water streams out through the gill slits, and the pharynx pushes the food through the esophagus into the stomach.

Since the plankton feeders are probably the most abundant of all fishes and are generally fairly small in size, they are the primary food source for the predator fishes such as the bluefish, thresher shark, giant tuna and others. Bluefish, in particular, are infamous for their bloodthirsty ferocity: they have often been reported attacking schools of menhaden or herring seemingly for the sheer sport of it, leaving a trail of bloody bits and pieces behind. Professor Spencer F. Baird, the first Commissioner of Fisheries in the United States, estimated that bluefish at the height of their abundance destroyed no less than 1,200 million millions of fishes each summer off the coast of southern New England alone—a statement that might be hard to prove but that nonetheless shows the powerful impression which the sight of a school of rampaging bluefish can leave on even a sober, scientific mind.

The thresher shark is a hardly less formidable predator, and one highly specialized for this form of hunting. Using its extremely long tail to lash the waters, it literally herds its prey of smaller, schooling fishes into a tight bunch, from which it can feed at leisure.

THE great sporting fishes, too, are predators, and so are some of the most important commercial fishes of the sea. The Atlantic tarpon shows a tiger's spirit when hooked and, since it may reach a length of eight feet and weigh as much as 340 pounds, is one of the most spectacular fighters of all. The black marlin is even bigger, reaching 15 feet and more than 1,000 pounds. The bluefin tuna is one of the biggest of all, weighing 1,800 pounds or more; its cousin, the yellowfin tuna, constitutes an important fishery in the Pacific Ocean.

The teeth of some carnivorous fishes are fearsome and specialized tools. Piranhas, for example, have teeth with cutting edges sharp as razors. The white shark grows teeth with serrated edges like steak knives, and still other fishes have teeth like needles that serve mainly to secure a firm grip on their prey. A few species of fish, like the wolf fish of the North Atlantic, the Port Jackson shark and the eagle ray, have developed massive crushing teeth to cope with the hard shells of mollusks.

Other fishes which also eat mollusks, like the cod, do not bother to crush their

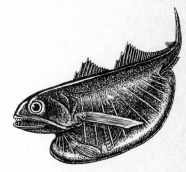
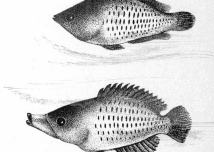

A LAKE IN WINTER

In winter, the water temperature of most Temperate Zone lakes is relatively uniform, ranging upward from 36° F. near the bottom to 32° F. at the frozen surface. Because of the almost uniform cold, fishes live at different levels than in summer. Catfish and bullheads hibernate in the shallows; bass and sunfish sink to moderate depths and feed little. Whitefish stay active near their summer level, and lively lake trout and perch continue to explore many levels in search of food.

shells at all, but simply swallow them whole and let their stomachs take care of them when the shells open up. In so doing, they unwittingly render valuable aid to scientists, for the stomach contents of such bottom dwellers often reveal species of mollusks that otherwise would not have been found.

Bottom-feeding fishes may be either carnivorous or herbivorous, but the majority are carnivorous as adults. Some are very catholic in their diet and some are very choosy. In either case, whether they are ground fishes that nose around on the bottom or predatory fishes that hunt at the surface, their jaws have become very specialized for their particular way of life. Sometimes they are telescopic, like those of the leaf fish, able to unfold and suck the prey in. In others, like the gray mullet and the gizzard shad, they are used simply to suck up the soft mud of the bottom and pass it through the stomach and intestine where animal and plant matter, living or dead, is extracted.

Most bottom fishes, except for a few like the carp and the parrotfish which chew their food, take what they get in one gulp, which occasionally leads to odd consequences. It is quite usual to see crabs, sea urchins and other spiny creatures inside the stomachs of fishes which have swallowed them whole.

Naturally, fishes will tend to congregate in the area where their particular food is most abundant, and this is the primary reason why both bottom fishes and surface dwellers are more plentiful close to the coasts, where plankton and bottom food are most readily available, rather than out in the deep ocean. Predatory fishes, by the same token, tend to follow the schooling fishes which are their normal prey. The type of food available in different localities will also obviously have a profound effect on the distribution of fishes. Those, for example, which prefer a soft diet, such as worms, will be found on muddy bottoms where the worms live, while those which prefer, say, a diet of cockles and clams will seek out a sandy bottom.

Beyond that, however, what prevents fishes from ranging any part of the great oceans in which most of them live? What, if anything, fences them in?

ONE would imagine that there are no boundaries in the sea and nothing to prevent any kind of fish, for example the cod or the herring of our temperate seas, from spreading all along the continental shelf into other climates. But the cod does not come much farther south than the British Isles in the eastern Atlantic and Virginia in the western Atlantic, and the herring does not come much farther south than the English Channel and Cape Cod. And as we go from temperate latitudes toward the tropics the number of species of fish increases, while the actual number of individuals becomes less, a pattern which follows that of animals on land.

The fact is that there are quite definite barriers to the unrestricted spread of animals in water. Among these, temperature is one of the most obvious and important, and the boundaries it imposes in the oceans are shown on maps as lines of equal temperature, or isotherms.

Compared to the variations we know on the land, the range of temperature in any body of water of any size is small. In any ocean, it generally varies no more than about 25° Fahrenheit. The hottest seas in the world are the Red Sea and the Persian Gulf, where temperatures of 86° F. occur. The coldest are in the Arctic and Antarctic, where a temperature as low as 28° F., four degrees below freezing, is not unusual. By comparison, extremes of temperature on land may range all the way from −126° F. on the Antarctic continent to 136° F. in the North African Sahara.

Except in high latitudes or cold weather, the temperature drops from the surface, where the water is always warmest—but it does not drop in even stages. In any sizable body of water there is usually a thermocline, or transitional zone, in mid-depth where the temperature falls rapidly in a relatively short distance. Below the thermocline temperatures change little the year round.

Smaller bodies of water naturally vary more widely in their seasonal temperatures than do the oceans, although very seldom do they reach that of the surrounding air. On the bottom, unless they freeze solidly in winter, temperatures are seldom less than 39° F.

Fishes are present in water of every temperature from the tropics to the poles, but they are most abundant in the temperate latitudes where temperatures range between about 43° F. and 68° F. Most fishes can put up with a fluctuation of 12° to 15° F. if the change is not effected too suddenly. Not surprisingly, the eggs and young are more sensitive to these fluctuations than the adults, which may often be found living in areas that are too warm or too cold for the eggs or fry.

THERE are, then, broad zones of temperature, each with its own kind of fishes which breed and grow best within its limits. And within these zones pretty much the same kinds of fishes live all around the globe.

The same thing is true of the organisms on which fishes feed. Planktonic organisms can be found all around the world in zones of similar temperature, but many die if they drift out of the favorable latitudes.

Between the lines of equal temperature there lies on either side of the equator, bounded by the line of 68° F., the tropical temperature zone with its own peculiar population of fishes. North and south of it are the north and south Temperate Zones, and between the lines of 68° F. and 54° F. is a transitional region where most of the tropical fishes gradually fade out, to be replaced by temperate ones. It is in this subtropical zone, along the western coasts of the continents, that the great shoals of pelagic fishes occur.

North of the 54° F. line we pass rather abruptly into the fish population of our own seas around the northern United States, Canada and northern Europe.

Because the great ocean currents surge through these areas, this line is not by any means a geographical one. However, it clearly delimits the areas of the great commercial ground-fish fisheries along the coast—the cod, halibut, haddock and redfish which have been exploited by many European nations since as early as 1504.

There is nothing fixed about these temperature zones; they may, and in fact occasionally do, shift drastically. Sometimes the changes that occur have a beneficial effect, as far as man is concerned. Since the early 1900s, for example, there has been a general warming-up over the whole North Atlantic, particularly near the Arctic Circle. The result has been a marked increase in the stocks of cod around Bear Island, Greenland and the north coast of Norway. British and Russian trawlers were naturally quick to take advantage of this change, and the trawl fishery around Bear Island really dates from this time.

There are other times, however, when changes in the temperature may have catastrophic results for the fishes. In 1882 the important tilefish fishery of southern New England was virtually wiped out by abrupt and major hydrographic changes. It is generally believed that unusually strong gales which swept that part of the Atlantic repeatedly during the winter temporarily flooded the bottom with abnormally cold water. In any case, an estimated 1.5 billion dead tilefish were seen floating on the surface of the ocean, and the total

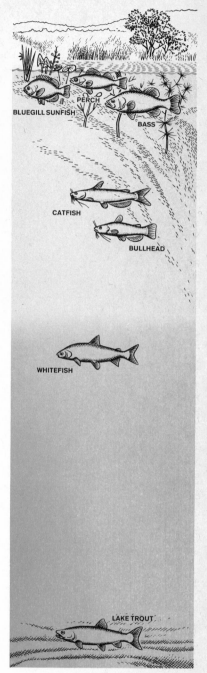

A LAKE IN SUMMER

In summer, warm air heats the surface of a lake, while the bottom water stays cold. Eventually a level is established where there is a sudden change from warm to cold. This area is called the thermocline. Sunfish, bass and perch are found in the warm upper levels, feeding on insects and small fish, while bullheads and catfish nose along the mud of the upper slopes and whitefish stay below the thermocline, where pressure and temperature suit them. Lake trout prefer the cold bottom water.

15

destruction was such that the fishery could not be re-established for many years.

Similarly, the shallow waters in the lagoons of Texas are occasionally so chilled by the unaccustomed low temperatures of abnormally cold winters that most of the fishes living in them are killed.

Off the coast of Peru catastrophes like this happen with some regularity, although they are not due to temperature changes alone but also to radical shifts in the supply of nutrients or the salinity of the water. The northward-flowing Humboldt, or Peruvian, Current off the west coast of South America is the chief supplier of nutrients in this area. The extreme richness of this current is due primarily to the upwelling of cold water from the ocean bottom, and the actual upwelling is produced largely by the action of the prevailing offshore winds, which drive the surface water away from the coast. The plankton thrives on this cold, rich water, and in turn serves as rich fodder for fishes, particularly the anchoveta, which are so abundant that in recent years Peru has captured the world's market in fish meal, exporting as much as 11 million tons of anchoveta in a single year.

There are years, however, when the winds diminish and the surface water as a consequence is not driven away from the coast. Then, at the time of what Peruvians call *El Niño*, the upwelling of cold water lessens and the surface layers warm up more than usually. The nutrients are quickly used up and soon the plankton dies. The millions of fishes that feed on it starve and die too, and finally the millions of birds that feed on the fishes. The piled-up, rotting corpses of fishes and birds cover the beaches and choke the coast for hundreds of miles, and the sterile sea turns foul with the decaying plankton.

SIMILAR disasters which occur from time to time off western Australia, in the Gulf of Mexico and in Africa, are due to the sudden bloom of great swarms of plankton—the so-called red tides. These catastrophes have received widespread publicity in Florida because of the trouble they sometimes cause in the tourist season, when they may litter the beaches for many miles with dead fishes. The red discoloration of the water which gives them their name is caused by a population explosion among tiny dinoflagellate members of the plankton. Red tides occur all over the world, and they generally follow a period of hot, windless days when the surface water becomes unusually warm. In this almost stagnant water dinoflagellates thrive enormously on certain salts, notably phosphates, which have accumulated at the surface. It has been stated often that what kills the fishes is suffocation through having their gills clogged by the sheer numbers of the plankton. The truth is that these dinoflagellates give off a toxin that is poisonous to many species. A red tide or something similar may have caused the widespread fish kill observed in 1957 by a Soviet research vessel cruising in the Arabian Sea. It reported millions of dead fishes over an area of 80,000 square miles between North Africa and India.

These are natural disasters of the sea and man can do little about them. Often less obvious but no less important to our fresh-water fisheries, however, is the loss of fish population because of the heedless pollution of rivers and streams with industrial wastes and raw sewage. Any significant change in the water in which a fish swims is likely to have serious consequences for the entire fish population, and the catastrophes that follow are a reminder that the balance of life in the waters of the world is often a precarious one, and that while we can still rejoice in the natural wealth of fishes numbering countless of millions, these same fishes may die in the millions too.

DULL COLOR AND A REEDLIKE BODY DISGUISE THESE BAY PIPEFISH, COUSINS TO THE SEAHORSE, AMONG WAVING CLUMPS OF EELGRASS

Fishes and Their Habitat

In adapting to the problems and opportunities of aquatic life, fishes have developed many ways of protecting and fending for themselves. Oldest of vertebrates, they now populate every part of their environment from mountain stream to ocean floor. The following pages show fishes that walk, crawl, fly, change color, look like rocks, wear armor, inject poison—and even fish for other fish.

DWELLERS IN TRANSPARENT TROPICAL WATERS, PORKFISH ARE BRIGHTLY COLORED BUT THEIR CORAL-REEF REALM HAS MANY HIDING PLACES

The Teeming Waters

Whether the earliest fishes lived in the sea or in fresh water is still a matter of discussion among scientists. But when they developed jaws and paired fins they invaded all parts of their world. Today there are at least 20,000 species, some chained to a special habitat, like the porkfish opposite and the rainbow trout at right, others far-roaming, like the salmon. Sea fishes like winter flounder and bluefish ride the tide into estuaries. The paintings on the four following pages show fishes in characteristic environments.

STREAMLINED BODIES give rainbow trout swimming speed. Trout live in cold, highly oxygenated water and adjust their color pattern to the amount of light and the color of the bottom.

The Varied Realms of the Fishes

FRESH-WATER FISHES

CREEK	LAKE AND RIVER	ESTUARY

The numbered fishes at right represent species in the painting on pages 20 and 21, and are colored to indicate their habitats: (1) brook trout; (2) stickleback; (3) white sucker; (4) golden shiner; (5) lamprey; (6) chain pickerel; (7) bluegill sunfish; (8) black-nosed dace; (9) smallmouth bass; (10) black crappie; (11) perch; (12) brown bullhead; (13) yellow bullhead; (14) lake trout; (15) white crappie; (16) eel; (17) burbot; (18) carp; (19) salmon; (20) great northern pike; (21) winter flounder; (22) young bluefish; (23) brown trout; (24) shad; (25) striped bass.

SALT-WATER FISHES

SURFACE	CONTINENTAL SHELF	CONTINENTAL SLOPE	DEEP SEA

In the key at right, the fishes painted on pages 22 and 23 are colored to show basic ocean realms: (1) hammerhead shark; (2) flyingfish; (3) manta; (4) mummichog; (5) tidewater silverside; (6) scup; (7) sculpin; (8) menhaden; (9) tautog; (10) bluefish; (11) halibut; (12) weakfish; (13) dolphin; (14) herring; (15) puffer; (16) dogfish; (17) tuna; (18) pollack; (19) cod; (20) haddock; (21) flounder; (22) searobin; (23) swordfish; (24) goosefish; (25) skate; (26) ocean pout; (27) chimaera; (28) *Photostomias guernei;* (29) hatchetfish; (30) lanternfish; (31) black swallower.

THE SCORPION FISH, a master of disguise, not only is able to take on the coloring of its surroundings but has added weedlike tabs to its head to blend with rocks and reefs where it waits in ambush for small fishes. It leads a sluggish existence but is dangerous if attacked, using its sharp, grooved dorsal spines like hypodermic needles to inject a stinging, paralyzing venom.

Many Forms for Many Uses

The bizarre fishes shown on these and the eight pages that follow have been shaped and colored with uncanny ingenuity to exploit their various underwater environments. The scorpion fish *(opposite)* and the yellow angler *(below)* lead sedentary lives and thus have no need for the streamlining of the far-roaming herring or marlin. Instead, they have come to resemble weed-grown rocks, both in form and color. Their disguises render them inconspicuous to their enemies and to the small fishes which they take by surprise and gulp whole. The searobin *(right)* is a more active fish which has become one of the most versatile of ocean dwellers. It can swim over the bottom and walk across it on leglike fins, but its reputation as a flier is quite unfounded.

THE SEAROBIN is well equipped for survival. Its large head is sheathed with bony plates, and it can use its pectoral rays to probe for food or, in time of danger, to cover itself with sand.

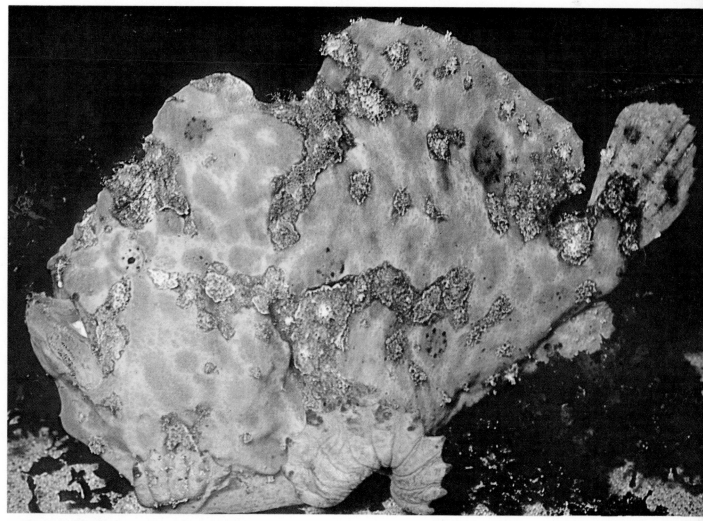

THE YELLOW ANGLER, camouflaged by an irregular shape and mock incrustations, creeps slowly across the ocean floor on armlike fins. A weak swimmer, it rarely pursues its prey but fishes for it instead. Its "pole," here hidden, is its first dorsal spine, its "bait" is a small, enticing flap of skin, which, dangling before its head, lures a fish right up to its waiting mouth.

TUBE MOUTH of the filefish contains protruding incisor teeth for nipping off barnacles which are crushed by teeth in the fish's throat. The filefish's skin is set with tiny scales and once served as sandpaper.

BOXLIKE ARMOR of the trunkfish, from which only its eyes, mouth and fins protrude, makes it an awkward and vulnerable swimmer. But its brilliant coloring is believed to warn predators that its flesh is poison.

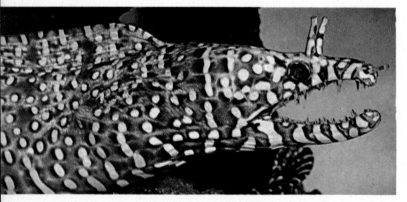

NEEDLE-SHARP TEETH of the dragon moray eel are offensive weapons added to an effective camouflage of broken stripes. By day it lies coiled in a hole in rock or coral; at night it strikes at unsuspecting fishes.

TRAILING FINS help this wispy young African pompano keep afloat. As they would serve no such purpose for the heavy adult, these fins gradually shorten while the fish matures.

AN ACTIVE HUNTSMAN, the archerfish (*above*) fires water at an insect by compressing its gill covers and forcing it through a tiny tube formed by its tongue and palate.

TARGET IS DOWNED and fish engulfs it—a cockroach (*right*). The archer's accuracy is the more amazing since it aims from under water and compensates for refraction.

FIERCE PREDATORS waiting for victims, spotted gars (*opposite*) hover motionlessly until the moment when they will slash at their prey, impaling it on sharp teeth.

SPEARLIKE BILL and a streamlined body make the giant blue marlin one of the sea's swiftest predators and greatest leapers. Marlins attain speeds of 40 to 50 miles an hour, and when hooked have been known to execute as many as 40 jumps. Rushing a school of fish, they strike out fiercely with their bills, then veer to feast on the maimed and dead.

30

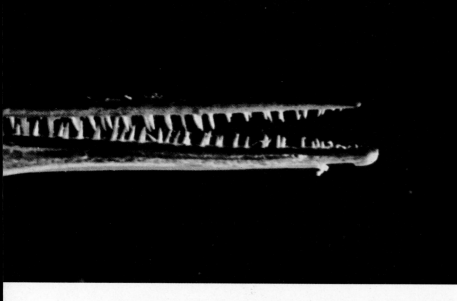

SCISSORLIKE JAWS, approximately one fifth the length of its cigar-thin body, enable the needlefish to snag victims on its sharply pointed teeth and juggle them around into a swallowing position. Swift and agile, needlefish have often been seen taking to the air in repeated leaps, hurdling floating objects apparently for sheer enjoyment of the sport.

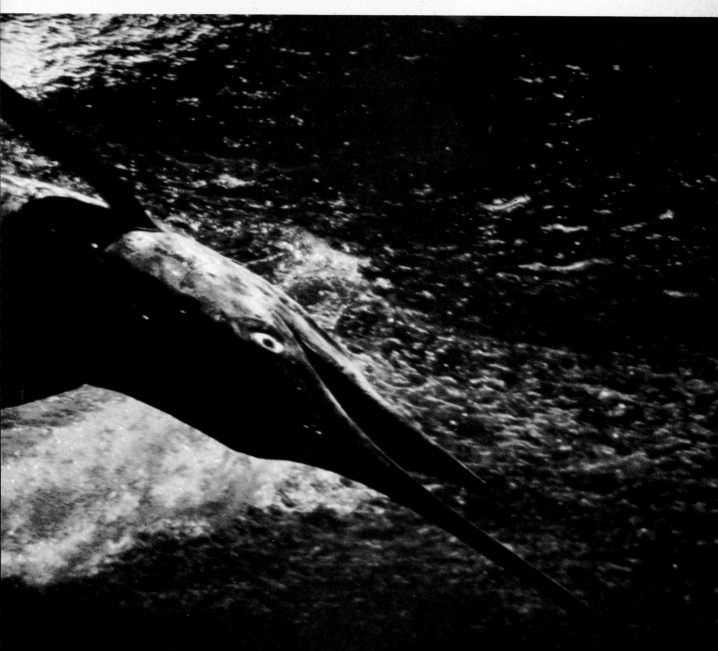

BENDING TO THE CURRENT, garden eels look like sinuously sprouting tendrils. They live in colonies but each is essentially a solitary, anchored almost all of its lifetime to a tube bored

in the sand. From these tubes they stretch a foot or more to
snatch food from the water, withdrawing if approached,
inch by inch, into their tubes until only sand is to be seen.

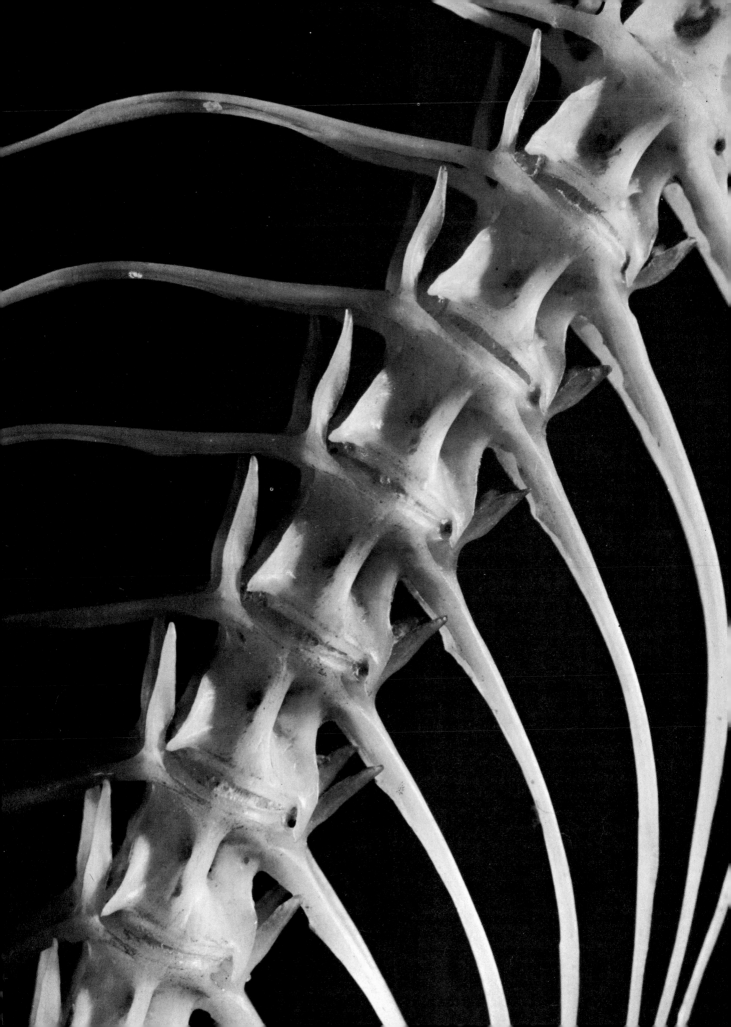

2

The Facts
of Life
in Water

To man, looking down into the water from his familiar warm world of light and air, the environment in which fishes dwell often seems cold, dark, mysterious and populated by creatures which in many cases are unique and weird. He himself can move about in it only with difficulty and in a very limited area, and the fact that he must equip himself with cumbersome gear in order to see, breathe, keep warm and propel himself at what must seem to fishes a creeping pace at best, tends to obscure some of the obvious advantages which fishes enjoy over creatures that live on land.

The fact of the matter is that there are advantages to living in water and they have played an important role in making fishes what they are. Water is not subject to sudden temperature changes, and is therefore an excellent habitat for a cold-blooded animal. The changes that do occur are slow and allow time for migration to more suitable climates or acclimatization to the existing one. The problem of supporting body weight, too, is far more simple than on land: since protoplasm has approximately the same density as water, a fish in its medium is almost weightless. This in turn means that it can get along with a light and simple bone structure; and it also practically removes any limit to its size, making it possible for a fish as huge as the whale shark to move about as easily and comfortably as a guppy.

Yet there is one basic difficulty which fish must cope with and which more than anything else has literally shaped their development—the fact that water is incompressible. Anyone who has ever waded in water that is more than ankle-deep has experienced the problem that fishes must overcome in moving: the water must be displaced, literally pushed aside, and just as quickly it closes in again from behind.

A flat and angular shape can be moved through such a medium only with difficulty (a board pushed straight down in water invariably slews off violently to one side or another), and for this reason fishes have a basic shape which is beautifully adapted to deal with this peculiarity of water. We call it streamlined: sharply pointed at the head, bulkiest in advance of the middle, tapering back so that the water can flow smoothly along the sides with a minimum of turbulence, even giving fast-moving fish a slight extra push as it closes in at the tail. There are variations of this shape, of course, but it is basic to all free-swimming fishes no matter in what specialized form they have evolved.

A FISH, like any vertebrate, is a bilaterally symmetrical animal, with its right and left sides mirror images. With all other vertebrates, it shares a simple basic anatomical plan—that of a hollow cylinder, open at both ends, with a food canal which runs from front to back inside. The front end represents the mouth, the back end the vent. Along the upper part of the body cylinder runs the vertebral column, a series of discs made of bone or cartilage which gives rigidity to the general body plan. Above the vertebral column and associated with it is a nerve cord, enlarged at the front end to form a coordinating center, or brain. From end to end the walls of the cylinder are divided into many similar segments repeating themselves from head to tail, and in these segments powerful locomotor muscles work upon the bone or cartilage skeleton, enabling the entire body to move in undulating motions from side to side.

The fact that fish are cold-blooded makes them, as previously noted, particularly well suited to life in the water, but it has its limitations too. When the water temperature changes beyond the limits they can tolerate, they have to move, a necessity which leads many of the Temperate Zone fishes to seasonal migrations. Should the temperature change abruptly and radically, the fishes may become too sluggish to escape and, unless conditions become more normal, they will die. Some fresh-water fishes, which in many cases cannot migrate when the seasons change, have circumvented this danger by going into a form of winter or summer sleep—they virtually stop feeding and remain inactive on the bottom in winter, or buried in the mud in summer, until the temperature turns favorable again.

The circulatory system of fishes is the simplest of all the vertebrates'. Basically, it is a straightforward cycle from the heart through the gills, where the blood is oxygenated, to the various organs and parts of the body which consume the oxygen, and back to the heart again. The heart itself is a pump with only two chambers, an auricle and a ventricle (as contrasted with the three-chambered heart of the amphibians, and four chambers in the mammals), which operates, figuratively speaking, in a direct line with the system.

A characteristic of fishes are the fins—the winglike structures, small or large, which give them stability in the water and aid them in moving and steering. Most fishes have two sets of paired fins—the pectorals, just behind the gills on

A KEY TO FISH GROWTH

Tiny scales first appear on most young fishes when they are from half an inch to an inch long. They do not increase in number, but grow as the fish grows. In summer, when food supplies are abundant, the fish grows rapidly, and so do its scales. In winter, growth slows and it is this difference that produces the clearly marked "rings," like those in tree trunks, on the scales, one for each year of the fish's life. The drawing above shows the annual rings on an enlarged haddock scale. The one below relates growth to scale size.

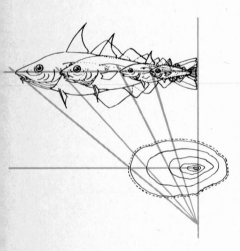

the side of the head, and the pelvics, usually located farther back. Along the mid-line on top is the dorsal fin, which may be subdivided into a spiny and a soft part; along the underside behind the vent is the anal fin. At the very back is the caudal, or tail fin.

All of these fins have their own particular functions in stabilizing and steering, and to accomplish these, they are movable, worked by muscles within the fish's body. The dorsals and pectorals, working together, are the basic stabilizing agents. The dorsal fins, standing straight up, act as antiroll stabilizers to keep the fish vertical; the pectorals, striking out sideways, are used for balancing and turning. The pelvic fins are used as stabilizers. The tail fin may be used to steer or, in the fastest fishes, as a stabilizer and a propelling agent, striking powerfully from side to side as the hind part of the fish's body undulates in the swimming motion. In fast-moving fishes the dorsal and anal fins fold flat when swimming, or even retract into little grooves so that they lie flush with the body.

In different types of fishes the fins may vary widely in placement and structure. Among most bottom dwellers, the paired fins are close together near the front, and the pelvics have shifted forward, sometimes even ahead of the pectorals to directly below the lower jaw, an arrangement that allows the head and gills to be held above the bottom. In other species the pelvic fins are vestigial, or have disappeared entirely, as in the eels. Among triggerfishes and other more-or-less disk-shaped species, the pectoral fins take over some or all of the propelling action. In the bottom-living searobin the pectorals have become disconnected "rays" that function like the legs of an insect. The lionfish, by contrast, has fins that serve chiefly as camouflage: long and feathery, they match the growth on coral rocks among which it lives.

The shapes of fishes vary widely too. Perhaps the most extraordinary change in shape has been adopted by those fishes which have taken to lying on the bottom: they have become flattened. Some lie on their bellies, and these have become flattened from above; others lie on their sides and have become flattened sideways. In these latter ones, the flattening takes place as the young fish grows, and results in the strange process of the eyes moving to the same, or upper, side of the head. Thus the flounder, for instance, which lies on its left side, has its eyes on the right side; its close cousin the fluke, on the other hand, has its eyes on the left side since it lies on its right side.

In the anglerfish group, the goosefish is one which has become flattened from above; it rarely moves, but angles for its prey with its own line and bait, a fleshy morsel hanging from a thin rod growing out of the top of its head. Its close relative, the frogfish, is somewhat more active: its pectoral fins have developed into a form of jumping fins with which it propels itself in hopping motions.

S KATES and rays are really sharks which have taken to lying on the bottom, and they too have become flattened from above. They move by undulations of their greatly enlarged side fins, which gives them the appearance of flying through the water. In many of them the tail is whiplike and has no motive power at all.

Even in the water, there are other ways of getting around than by swimming and, in varying degrees, fishes have taken to them all. They crawl on the bottom, like the searobin and the gurnard, and can even crawl right out of the water onto the beach, as the mudskipper does. The Malayan climbing perch and the Chinese snakehead travel unconcernedly overland from pool to pool by wriggling along exactly the way most fishes swim. The climbing perch keeps

HOW A FISH SWIMS

For a fish to move through water, which is incompressible, it must actually shove it aside. Most fishes can do this by wiggling back and forth in a snakelike motion. The fish pushes water aside by the forward motion of its head, first to the left and then the right, and also with the curve of its body and its flexible tail. The water, returning to its original position, now flows back along the fish's narrowing sides, closing in at the tail and helping the fish forward. The blue outlines of this dogfish show one body stroke.

its deep, narrow body from tipping over by using its pectoral fins as props.

Some fish can take to the air, if only for short distances. The garfish skitters along the surface using its tail like the propeller of an outboard motor. But flyingfish really fly—they can skim above the water for nearly a minute and, if there is a good breeze to lift them up, they may reach a height of 10 to 20 feet, planing from wave to wave with their greatly expanded forefins held rigidly out like wings. There are biplane flyingfish that use both their pelvics and pectorals, monoplane types that use the pectorals only, and even a freshwater species that flies like a bird, flapping its pectorals as it skims across the water's surface.

ONE striking characteristic of fish is immediately apparent: they are covered from head to tail in a generally flexible armor of rounded overlapping plates of bone. These scales are embedded in the inner, or foundation, layer of the skin, and they form an important protective covering. In addition to its basic armor of scales, a fish is further protected by a layer of mucous slime. Produced by many invisible glands scattered all over the body, this mucus is antiseptic, helping to keep off fungi and bacteria as well as lubricating the body surface. In size and thickness, scales may vary greatly, from those of the mahseer, a fish of Indian rivers that grows up to 12 feet long and has scales as large as a man's hand, to the microscopic ones of the common eel. A very few species, like the lamprey, have no scales at all. In other fishes, like the trunkfish, they have fused to form an inflexible, boxlike covering or, as in the pipefish and seahorse, rows of connected bony plates.

Scales grow as the fish grows, and especially in fishes of the Temperate Zones they leave a distinctive record of age and seasons. New growth is laid down by the layer of skin which covers them on the outside, forming all around the edges. Since in the Temperate Zones each scale grows fastest during the summer, when the fish is getting the most food, it is sometimes possible to tell a fish's age by counting the growth rings on its scales.

A fish's mouth is its one and only tool for feeding, and as a result it is highly adapted in all types of fish for the job it has to do. The parrotfish, as mentioned earlier, has developed a regular beak to snip off plants and coral animals; the little sand launce has a digging tool, a hard, sharp projection on its lower jaw, with which to root around in the sand for its food of small crustaceans, fish fry

TYPES OF SCALES

The four kinds of scales shown here represent the body armor of all of today's fishes. The primitive placoid scales found in sharks, rays and skates are toothlike structures, each about the size of a grain of coarse sandpaper, which the shark's skin resembles. They cover most of the body, including the head, but are separated from each other by a layer of skin which is tough and liberally sprinkled with star-shaped pigments. Ganoid scales are present in a few primitive bony fishes, like the gar. Diamond-shaped and attached to each other by joints, these scales are coated with ganoin, a substance that gives a look of polished ivory.

The most common scales are called ctenoid and cycloid. They differ in one respect only: the former has a comblike edge, while the latter has a rounded border. Most bony fishes like herring, salmon and bass have one or the other of these types of scales. They are arranged in overlapping rows and, because they are thin, light and flexible, most fishes that have them are mobile and fast-moving.

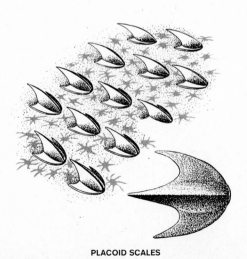

PLACOID SCALES

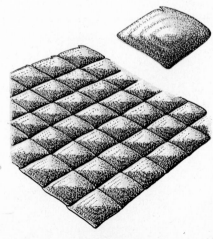

GANOID SCALES

and occasional worms. Fishes that feed at the surface generally have upturned mouths, occasionally with greatly lengthened lower jaws like the halfbeak. Similarly, bottom dwellers like the angler and stargazer, which feed on prey that swims above them, have mouths that are turned upward. On the other hand, those that feed off the bottom, like the skates and rays, the haddock and the common sucker, have their mouths on the underside of their heads.

How does a fish breathe? We know that, like any animal, it needs oxygen to sustain life—and in fact its breathing process is not so very different from that of air-breathing animals. Oxygen is dissolved in water, and fish extract it by taking water through their mouths, passing it through gill chambers and expelling it finally through openings in the sides of the head. The gills function very much like lungs. They are lined by blood vessels close to the surface, covered by thin skin. The skin forms folds and plates, the so-called gill filaments, so as to increase the absorptive area. The entire gill mechanism is compactly contained in a chamber under the protection of a bony shield, the operculum, or gill cover.

The gill mechanism is a highly adaptable one—so much so that a few fishes can even use atmospheric air as well as water to obtain the oxygen they need. The common carp, for example, when its pond runs short of oxygen or dries up in the hot summer months, takes in a bubble of air and holds it in its mouth near its moist gills. The climbing perch, the snakehead and the Indian catfish have special air chambers with folded walls near the gills. Lungfishes have, for all practical purposes, perfectly good lungs, with blood vessels arranged on the same pattern as those of the amphibian frogs and newts. In some archaic fishes, the primitive lung which later developed into the gas bladder (also called swim or air bladder) is still connected to the gullet, and in consequence such fishes, like the gar and the bowfin, have, in effect, emergency lungs.

THE gas bladder in those modern fish which are equipped with it, however, no longer has a breathing function but acts like a very sophisticated balloon. Built into the gut cavity underneath the spine, it is an airtight sac lined with glands that can selectively take gases directly from the fish's blood stream and put them in the bladder. The amount of gas is precisely regulated to give the fish just the amount of buoyancy it needs to remain at whatever level it may dwell, whether near the surface or deeper down to about 200 fathoms. Many fishes which live in the deeper regions of the sea, as well as most bottom-dwelling

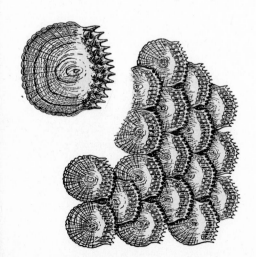

CTENOID SCALES

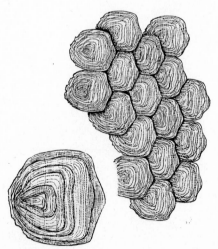

CYCLOID SCALES

fishes, have no use at all for a gas bladder and hence do not develop one.

Gas bladders have a limiting effect on a fish's depth range, since adjustment to depth and pressure takes place only slowly. Most fishes that normally live at depth cannot rise to the surface without the bladder expanding beyond the size the fish can tolerate—if it is caught on a hook and line and brought all the way up, the bladder may blow up to such a size that it forces the stomach out through the mouth. Certain fishes like those of the mackerel family have a very small gas bladder or none at all and hence no such limitation. They can forage for food at various depths. The price they pay, however, is that they must be constantly on the move to keep from sinking.

THERE are some fishes that pass regularly between salt water and fresh water, and they have special problems—chemical barriers which they have to surmount. Living in water as it does, a fish must maintain a balance between the salts in its blood and body fluids and those which may—or may not—be present in the water around it. A fresh-water fish has a higher salt content in its body fluids than does the surrounding water, and since the water seeks constantly to dilute these salts by entering its body through the skin, gill membranes, mouth and other exposed body surfaces, it is under relentless pressure of a water invasion. To keep the proper balance, therefore, it constantly excretes water. The marine fish, on the other hand, has the opposite problem: it is constantly losing water to its saltier environment, and to maintain its proper chemical balance it must gulp water steadily lest it shrivel up like a prune. To cope with the salinity of the water they take in, marine fishes have cells in the gill filaments whose particular function it is to excrete certain of these salts.

Water being such an entirely different environment from air, we may well wonder how the senses of a fish operate to keep it informed of where it is and what is going on around it. What does a fish see? How does it hear? Does it have a nose to smell with as we do, a sense of taste, of touch?

The answer is that fishes have all of these five senses—and one more, a true sixth sense which makes them acutely aware of very subtle changes in the flow of water around them. This sixth sense is unique to them and it operates by means of nerve organs located in a canal system underneath the skin.

To begin with the sense of sight, however, it functions in fishes much as it does in human beings—with the difference that a good many fishes which find their food above the surface of the water must cope with the phenomenon of refraction. This bending of light which occurs when light rays pass from air to water or vice versa causes an object seen, for example, in the bottom of a bathtub or a trout pool to appear to be displaced unless it is viewed directly from above. Thus a man fishing with a bow and arrow has to aim considerably below the image of the fish he is shooting at if he is going to hit it—and by long practice he learns to do so. Similarly, a trout or bass or salmon rising to strike at an insect flitting above its pool has to leap out of the water some distance ahead of the target it sees—and long, long ago it developed this art through the process of evolution to the point where it is now a sure, instinctual skill.

Fishes which find their prey in the water do not have to cope with this aspect of the problem of refraction, for light under water travels, just as it does in the air, in a straight line. There are, however, other factors which affect the mechanics of seeing in their underwater world, and hence the structure of their eyes. Chief among these are the amount of light available to see by and the limit of vision imposed by the fact that even the clearest water is much less clear than air.

The absence of brilliant light in the underwater world has led to one important simplification of eye structure in most fishes as compared with the eyes of terrestrial or air-borne animals: they can get along with little or no contraction of the iris. (They can do without eyelids, too, since the water in which they live constantly washes their eyes and keeps them free of foreign matter.) They have an iris, a metallic-looking ring around the dark pupil, but it does not need to widen or shrink as much as ours to regulate the amount of light passing into the eye. Because of this, in most fishes the iris is virtually inflexible.

The fact that vision under water is, at best, limited to about 100 feet—and often a great deal less—also makes it unnecessary for fishes to accommodate their eyes to widely varying distances. Most of the time, they need to see objects at only fairly close range, and their eyes are built accordingly. Their lenses are not gently rounded and adjustable in curvature like human eyes, but are spherical and rigid. At rest, the fish's eye is set to see objects in the immediate foreground; if it needs to look further into the distance, the entire lens is pulled backward in the eye by a special muscle called the *retractor lentis*.

THERE is another, more important reason for the spherical shape of a fish's lens, and this has to do, again, with refraction. Since the lens is filled with a liquid of almost the same density as water, there is no refraction of light passing from the water outside the eye through the watery substance inside the lens —and by the laws of optics this means that the lens must be sharply curved to focus an image on the retina. The sharpest curve that a fish can attain is a sphere, and hence its spherical lens. Even this, some scientists believe, may not be enough to give it a really well-focused picture, which is why a fish, even under the best of circumstances, may never get a really clear look at things under water.

However, fishes do have an advantage that terrestrial animals do not—they can see in more than one direction at a time. Their eyes are placed on the sides of their heads, rather than in the front, and what each eye sees is registered on the opposite side of the brain—i.e., objects on the right register on the left side of the brain and vice versa.

This gives the fish monocular vision, which has its limitations, particularly in judging distance. But there is good reason to believe that straight ahead there is a relatively narrow area in which both eyes see simultaneously, giving the fish a measure of binocular vision—and hence a sense of perspective—just as we have. And indeed, it would appear that a fish does try to make up for the monocular vision of its individual eyes by whirling around, if something attracts its attention off to one side, so that the object is brought into the narrow common field of vision of both eyes where its distance can be better estimated. Thus what it sees with one eye only may register on the opposite side of its brain merely as a stimulus to turn and get both eyes into play straight ahead.

To what degree fishes can see colors is not known. The general tone of the fish's submarine world is greenish-blue, since other colors are absorbed and disappear only a short distance from the surface. Color perception, therefore, is not of great importance to any except surface-swimming fishes. We do know, however, that all fishes except the shark can see some color. Microscopic examination of the nerve cells in their eyes has shown that they are supplied with visual cones, the nerve cells which differentiate between colors, and visual rods, which are used mainly at night.

To what extent fishes can use color in their daily existence is, however, still a mystery. Some show preference for one color over another, as trout seem to

THE STRUCTURE OF GILLS

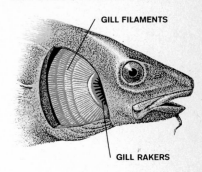

The head of a cod with the gill covering removed reveals the gill filaments arranged in overlapping fan-shaped rows. At the base of the gill filaments, just behind the fish's mouth cavity, are the gill rakers.

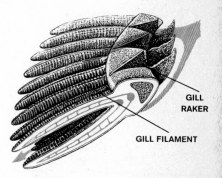

A close-up shows the course water takes (arrows) as it passes the rakers and flows over and between the filaments. The rakers strain out most food particles. Edible solids are swallowed; others are coughed up.

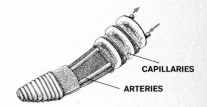

An enlarged filament tip shows blood (arrows) flowing through tiny vessels (capillaries) where oxygen and carbon dioxide exchange occurs. The vessels are linked to arteries which carry the blood to the body.

A FISH'S FIELD OF VISION

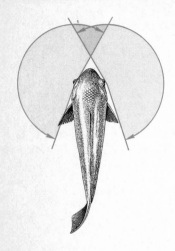

The eyes of most fishes are placed so widely apart that they are considered to have monocular vision, that is to say, each eye collects a separate, uncoordinated image which overlaps little, if at all, with the other. In addition, the retinas of a fish (below) pass impulses only to the side of the brain opposite the eye, enhancing the monocular effect. But man (bottom) has a double advantage: (1) his eyes are placed in front of his head, giving him a wide field of overlapping vision (90°); and (2) his eyes send simultaneous impulses along nerves to both sides of his brain, making for true binocular vision.

distinguish between the colors of different flies. Again, if a spectrum is shone into a darkened aquarium the fish will go for the green and yellow bands and remain in them, while if only a red light is used they behave as though they were in the dark.

Bright or strongly contrasting colors, of course, might be useful to fishes among themselves as a means of identifying certain of their species—but here again, we are not sure to what degree this may be true. Certainly some tropic fish are clad in such brilliant contrasting patterns that it seems logical to assume they must have some significance to other creatures of the submarine world. Is the pilotfish, for example, recognized by the shark because of the strong vertical bars on its dark back and sides? That might explain why this little fish, only some nine inches long, can fearlessly swim along with its far larger and voracious companion and yet never be mistaken for food.

It may also be that brilliant hues are a warning to indicate that a fish is unpalatable or poisonous. There are some fishes which never seem to be eaten by other fishes, and in the shallow waters of tropical coral reefs where underwater visibility is relatively high, their colors, setting them off so strongly from their fellows, may be their protection.

In any case, it does seem likely that certain color patterns are recognized by fish of the same species as distinctive identifying liveries. A flash of bright color in their greenish-blue world may be more quickly apparent than a dimly seen shape moving in and out of range. Supporting this theory is the fact that many species which typically travel in shoals, staying close together, seldom have dazzle patterns, while those which live isolated, scattered among rather uniformly colored surroundings, generally have the striking kind of livery which others of their kind can recognize instantly.

The colors themselves in most fishes are formed by a layer of cells in the skin underneath the transparent scales. These cells are called chromatophores, or color bearers, and contain granules of pigment which may be of various kinds.

Firstly, there are orange, yellow or red pigments of the same type as those which give flowers their red or yellow colors. Secondly, there are black pigments which are really waste products of the body and are found in many other parts besides the skin (the internal organs of a black-skinned fish are generally black too). Lastly, fishes have a reflective substance called guanin, carried in the form of crystals that, according to their quantity and distribution, result in white, silver or iridescent hues. A combination of guanin and black pigment produces metallic blue and green reflections.

Protection is, of course, a major factor in the color scheme of most fishes. The "obliterative" patterns of fish which live in the upper layers of the sea—dark on the back, white or silver on the belly—make them difficult to see from any direction. Bottom fishes show really elaborate camouflages—their colors may match the bottom or, like the zigzag paint on old-time warships, tend to break up the fish's outline. To such "disruptive" color schemes still another is added which appears to change the fish's shape completely, a so-called "deceptive" scheme.

Sometimes the background is matched to the point of imitating it in pattern as well as color. The Amazon leaf fish exactly resembles a leaf floating in the water. A fish will even change its camouflage at various stages of its life—in tropical waters around Florida, for instance, a number of fishes, when quite young, take on the shape and color of the pods of mangrove seeds lying on the white sand where they live, but when they outgrow the mangrove pods, so to speak, this disguise is useless, and they move into deeper water and develop a banded pattern. The common flounder is one of the best camouflage artists of all, and can match pebbles, sand or dark mud with chameleonlike ease.

Camouflage can even go so far as to involve modification of the fish's structure. The sargassum fish is covered with filaments and small flaps that imitate the weed in which it lurks, and the ribbon seahorse has long tendrils like the blades of sea grass to which it clings.

Most fishes keep the same general color scheme throughout life, but some change color from youth to maturity. Young salmon and trout show dark stripes which they lose when full-grown. The male salmon, trout, stickleback and many others also change color at the breeding season. Dr. William Beebe once found some coral fishes which showed as many as seven variants of the same color pattern within 24 hours.

Even the sexes may dress up in different colors. The male dragonet and cuckoo wrasse are as colorful as birds of bright plumage, while the females of both species are dull. Other fish, again, darken at night or, like the barracuda, take on a different pattern entirely. Many fish change color when frightened, as when they are hooked.

On death the colors of fish generally change at once and are often quite different from those they had in life. Perhaps the most extraordinary death changes are those shown by the lively green and gold dolphin, or dorado. In its final throes the green and gold turn to blue and chalk-white and then slowly, after the last quiver of life has ceased, to a dull, opaque olive drab.

A great deal of study has been devoted to the question of whether fishes can hear in our sense of the word. It has been held that they cannot—what there is of the ear as we know it seems to be purely a balancing organ. However, since a number of fish do make noises under water which seem to be breeding signals, follow-my-leader calls or recognition signals, it does seem logical to suggest that fishes may perceive sound in some way. The likeliest explanation is that they sense sound waves, using the gas bladder as a resonator. While there is no eardrum and inner ear bone structure, which constitute the true hearing apparatus of the higher animals, it has been suggested that the gas bladder and the so-called Weberian ossicles, a series of small bones connecting the gas bladder to the inner ear area in certain fishes, may function like an ear in detecting sound in the form of vibrations. Certainly some fishes are extremely sensitive to vibrations which involve direct movement of the water—they can detect the beat of a ship's propeller at a great distance, and a footstep on the riverbank, shaking the earth ever so slightly and thus setting the water in motion as well, is enough to disturb the trout in its pool.

T HE sense of touch is conveyed to fishes by small, sensitive nerve organs scattered over the skin. These are particularly abundant around the head and lips, and many fish even carry them on feelers called barbels. The cod and the surmullet have fairly short barbels under their chins with which they probe over the ground; catfish have very long ones, like whiskers.

It is characteristic of almost all fishes that their sense of smell is developed to a very high degree. Fishes have the equivalent of our nostrils, a pair of small pits opening to the outside, only on the snout. Inside they are lined with folded walls, providing a maximum of absorptive surface, which contain the nerve cells that communicate smell.

The sense of smell in most fishes is so acute that they seem to use it more than

DIVIDED VISION

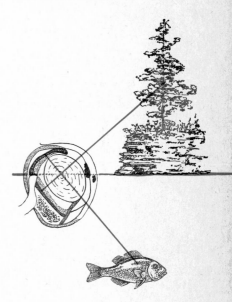

The eyeball of the Anableps, a small fish of Central and South American rivers, is adapted to seeing both below and above the surface simultaneously. This picture shows its ability to see a tree on the bank and a predatory fish deep in the water equally well. Each eye of this so-called "four-eyed" fish is located on top of its head in such a way that it can swim with half of the eye out of the water, occasionally ducking to moisten the aerial sections.

sight in seeking out their food. Sharks can smell blood a long way off and will materialize seemingly out of nowhere to attack a bleeding fish or animal. Using chopped-up fish or fish blood is an effective way of attracting, or "chumming," bluefish or other game fishes. Lampreys will react if just a cupful of water in which other fish have been swimming is poured into their tank: they instantly become alert and try to trace the origin of this sudden delicious aroma.

As for the sense of taste, it is probably not an important one in any fish's life. To begin with, none of them except lungfishes have taste organs in their mouths. They do have taste buds, but these may be located on the head, body, tail, modified fins or chin barbels, so that if they do taste food, they do so before taking it into their mouths. Most fish simply gulp their food directly into the stomach, where it is digested.

T HE most extraordinary of the senses which fish have is that unique sixth sense which is so delicately attuned to movements and currents in the water. The minute system of canals in the skin from which it is gained can be quite clearly seen on the sides of the fish as a file of scales shaped differently from the others. This is called the lateral line. At intervals in the main canal may be found highly specialized sense organs. Other similar canals, also equipped with these sense organs, branch over the head and face.

Scientists have yet to discover all the secrets of the lateral line, but it is clear that its basic function is associated with monitoring the flow of water. Cutting the base of the branch nerve which leads from it to the brain, for example, obviously affects the fish's ability to react to disturbances in the water or changes in the direction of flow. Thus it is possible to conclude that this special sense enables a coral fish, for example, to dart like lightning into a small crevice it cannot possibly see clearly, or a fish in turgid water to turn away from obstacles still invisible in the murk. And it may also be the lateral line which enables vast shoals of fish, comprising thousands of individuals, to hold such perfect formations as they swim along.

Anyone who has ever fished or watched a fisherman has wondered whether fish feel pain. This is a very difficult question to answer satisfactorily; pain is a psychological as well as a physical reaction, and there is no way of learning from the fish just what it feels. We may be fairly certain, however, that fishes do not experience the psychological component of pain; there is little evidence that they learn by experience or association as we do.

Do they, then, feel pain physically? Pain is experienced by the brain as the result of information conveyed to it by the nerves. In the human brain it is the cortex which integrates the messages conveyed by the sensory nerves and those conveyed to the motor nerves; and it is the cortex which produces pain. But fish have no structure comparable to the human cortex, and there is no other part of their brain which appears to perform this function.

The amount of sensory stimulation required to produce pain is called the pain threshold. It is much higher in some animals, and in some individuals, than in others. The lower we go in the evolutionary scale the higher the pain threshold becomes, the more stimulation is required before a pain reaction can be observed. We may be pretty certain that it is high indeed in fish. They seem to react to excessive stimulation merely by moving—or trying to move—away.

This is why a fish can swim off apparently unconcerned with a hook in its mouth or a harpoon in its back, and a wounded shark will continue to attack even while its companions are tearing at its bowels.

LIKE A MUSEUM MODEL, THE TRANSPARENT BODY OF THE GLASS CATFISH REVEALS EVERY DETAIL OF SKELETON, BRAIN AND INTERNAL ORGANS

Mechanics of Adaptation

The delicate structure of the crystalline little fish swimming above is the product of millions of years in water. While other vertebrate descendants of the fishes modified their bodies for life on land and in the air, the fishes themselves remained in their dense and in-compressible medium. Some of the fascinating ways they adapted themselves to its peculiar laws are shown on the following pages.

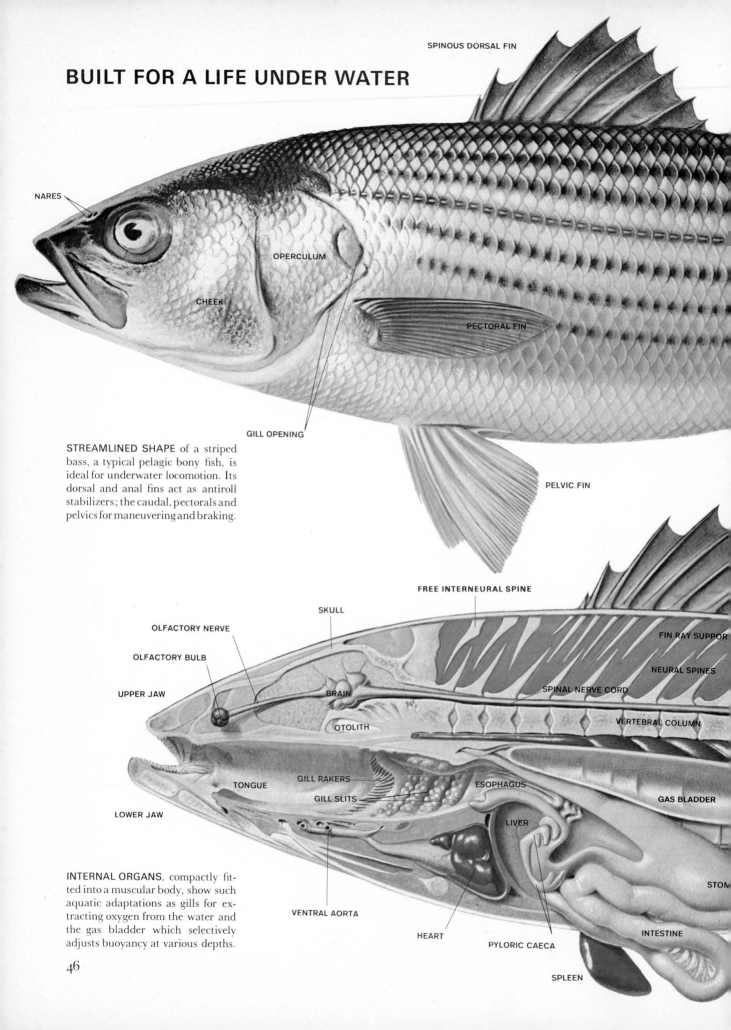

BUILT FOR A LIFE UNDER WATER

SPINOUS DORSAL FIN

NARES

OPERCULUM

CHEEK

PECTORAL FIN

GILL OPENING

PELVIC FIN

STREAMLINED SHAPE of a striped bass, a typical pelagic bony fish, is ideal for underwater locomotion. Its dorsal and anal fins act as antiroll stabilizers; the caudal, pectorals and pelvics for maneuvering and braking.

FREE INTERNEURAL SPINE

SKULL

OLFACTORY NERVE

OLFACTORY BULB

UPPER JAW

FIN RAY SUPPOR

NEURAL SPINES

BRAIN

SPINAL NERVE CORD

OTOLITH

VERTEBRAL COLUMN

TONGUE

GILL RAKERS

GILL SLITS

ESOPHAGUS

LOWER JAW

GAS BLADDER

LIVER

INTERNAL ORGANS, compactly fitted into a muscular body, show such aquatic adaptations as gills for extracting oxygen from the water and the gas bladder which selectively adjusts buoyancy at various depths.

VENTRAL AORTA

STOM

HEART

PYLORIC CAECA

INTESTINE

SPLEEN

46

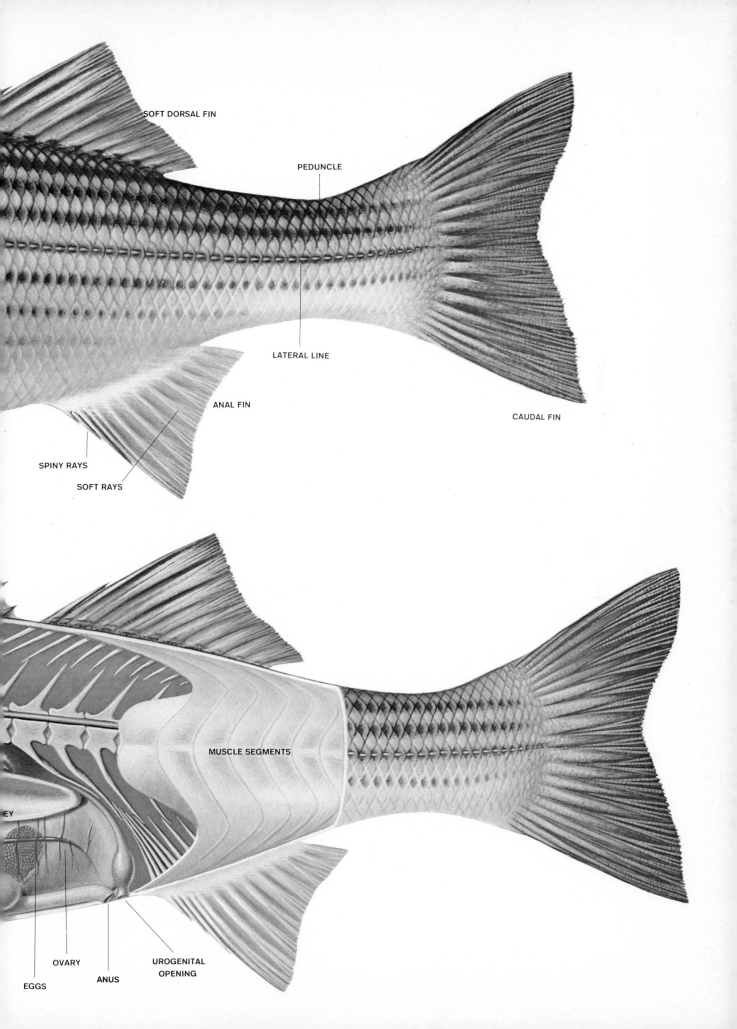

SOFT DORSAL FIN

PEDUNCLE

LATERAL LINE

ANAL FIN

CAUDAL FIN

SPINY RAYS

SOFT RAYS

MUSCLE SEGMENTS

EY

OVARY

ANUS

UROGENITAL
OPENING

EGGS

A BRILLIANT ANGELFISH, native of coral reefs off the west coast of Mexico, wears a dazzling livery. Its sunburst hues, outlining fin and scale pattern, are formed by color cells of red and yellow pigments. The typical white band is due to guanine crystals, originating from a waste product of blood; the blue to crystals overlying black and other pigment cells.

CROSS SECTION through the skin of a sailfin molly shows a thin outer layer covering the inner skin in which scales are embedded. Black pigment cells overlie the reddish muscle tissue.

Many-Colored Suits of Armor

The scaly and often colorful armor of a fish is ideal for protecting it in its watery environment. The scales themselves, tough and overlapping, form an effective shield against injury. Their translucent quality, furthermore, permits the fish to assume all sorts of different color schemes. He can be bold and brilliant or drab and self-effacing; he can present a pearly white aspect from below when seen against the light surface, or blend with the shifting blues and greens of the sea itself when viewed from above. At mating time, he can don bright hues; in other circumstances, to protect himself, he can vary his colors from hour to hour, matching his different backgrounds. Under the stress of excitement, he sometimes changes colors right before our eyes. All of these little miracles of color take place in his skin, by means of versatile pigment cells and crystals.

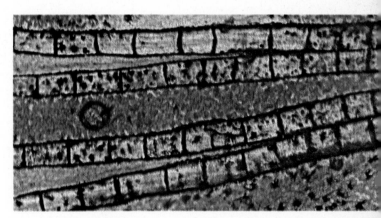

COLOR CELLS, magnified in a photomicrograph, dot the caudal fin of a sailfin molly with red, yellow and black. The black material is melanin, a waste product of the fish's body.

How a Fish Sees

Any small boy knows that seeing under water is a different matter from seeing in air. Light is diffused and quickly fades to a dim twilight zone. Even in clear water, only relatively close objects can be sharply focused. But this is the environment which the eyes of fishes must cope with, and their adaptations for the liquid medium are most ingenious. Their primary need is to see movements and nearby shapes—and this they do to

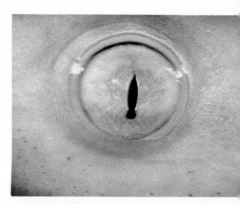

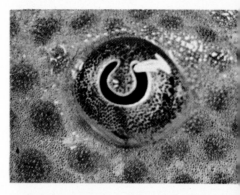

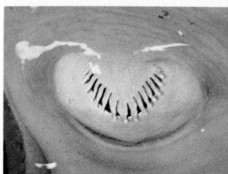

MONOCULAR VISION is demonstrated by a wrasse whose right eye peers forward to see what lies ahead while the left eye looks off to the side. Linked individually to the brain, each eye transmits its message for action, regardless of what the other sees.

SLIT PUPIL of black-tipped shark (*top*) controls light, but armored catfish (*center*) and skate (*bottom*) use a form of eyeshade.

perfection, as the fisherman casting for a wary trout knows well. With their eyes set on the sides of their head, many of them can register practically everything that moves around them at any time. Needing no eyelids or tear ducts in their liquid medium, they have evolved ways of coping with varying amounts of light (*below*, *opposite*), and some have even camouflaged their eyes to blend with the rest of their bodies (*below*).

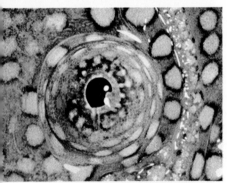

WHITE BANDS hide eyes of cardinal fish (*top*), but the southern stargazer (*center*) and wrasse blend theirs with their bodies.

EYES ON STALKS are used by Asia's celestial telescope goldfish to look upward in a fixed stare. Set on bulbous projecting outgrowths of the head, such telescopic optics are good light collectors but can usually serve only for upward or forward vision.

THE LONG CANINE TEETH OF THE BARRACUDA, A FEROCIOUS PREDATOR OF THE SEA, ARE SPECIALIZED FOR SEIZING VICTIMS, AFTER WHICH SMALL

THE FLEXIBLE TUBE SNOUT of the birdfish indicates it is a bottom feeder. This colorful wrasse is plentiful in Hawaiian waters.

THE TROWEL-LIKE LOWER JAW of the Ubangi mormyrid is used to probe the bottom mud for worms, insects and other food.

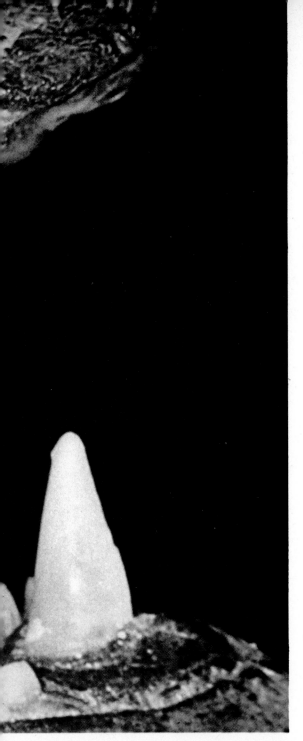

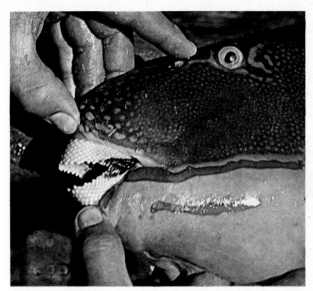

BEAKLIKE JAWS and fused platelike teeth of the parrotfish are for snipping off pieces of seaweed or coral and crushing them.

Jaws and Teeth for Every Need

All of the myriad life of the waters serves as food for some fish or another. Predators devour other fishes, bottom browsers crack mollusks, crustaceans and corals for the tasty morsels within, and a host of others swimming between the bottom and the surface dine on worms, insects and plankton strained from the richly nutritious meadows of the sea. To help them in gathering their food, fishes have developed many varieties of jaws and mouths and teeth. The mouths may be specialized as vacuum cleaners, the jaws as scoops or shovels. Fishes have no limbs to help in grasping food, so their teeth must be able to seize and cut, or tear and crush whatever is taken. For these varied purposes, many fishes have teeth not only in their jaws but on their tongues, their palates and even far back within their throats.

GGER-EDGED TEETH CUT THE PREY INTO RIBBONS FOR FEEDING

THE WEIRD WOLF EEL, a giant of the blenny family, has canine teeth in the front of its jaws and massive grinders in the back.

THE SUCKERMOUTH CATFISH aims its vacuum-cleaner jaws downward, using tiny teeth to scrape vegetation from bottom.

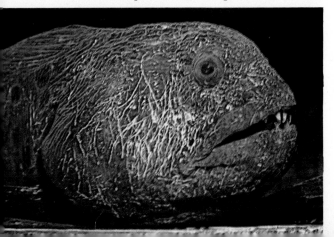

The Vital Need for Oxygen

The necessity of obtaining the oxygen which they, like all other creatures, must have to live presents the fishes with special problems that they have solved in special ways. Their primary oxygen source, of course, is the surrounding water, and their primary breathing apparatus is their gills. But should the water be deficient in oxygen, due to pollution or any other cause, some can come to the surface and, to a limited degree, gulp down air like any landlubber, taking the life-giving element direct from the atmosphere. Goldfish can be observed doing this when their tank is too small or when their water is contaminated with decaying food. But only a few fishes can live on atmospheric oxygen for any length of time, and in streams, small lakes and ponds nothing is more deadly to them than waste products dumped into the water, fouling the liquid environment and tying up the precious oxygen in the chemistry of decay.

Certain fishes do have auxiliary breathing mechanisms in addition to their gills. Lungfishes breathe air by using the gas bladder, which also serves as an emergency oxygen tank for the Amazon's giant redfish. Other species, like bettas and climbing perches, store air in chambers above their gills. The mudskipper carries a mouthful of air and water when it ventures ashore to feed (*opposite, below*).

BREATHING APPARATUS of a typical fish, the king mackerel, shows the gill arches with the gills on their back edges and the fringes of the gill filaments, darkened by rich blood vessels.

TORPEDO BATFISH breathes like any other fish by drawing water into its mouth and over its gills. But because its shape is so modified, its gill openings have been relocated (*right*).

VIEWED FROM THE REAR, the batfish shows gill openings located behind the big pectoral fins, rather than in front of them. An additional advantage is a jet effect as water is expelled.

SURFACING FOR AIR, a rich-hued Siamese fighting fish has just expelled bubbles of vitiated air *(upper right)* and is about to take a fresh supply which it will store in a pair of internal chambers above the gills. Filled with thin plates covered with fine blood vessels, these extra breathing organs provide for a direct exchange of oxygen and waste gases, as in our lungs.

ABSORBING OXYGEN through a dense network of blood vessels from the air and water carried in its swollen jowls, the mudskipper can leave the water to forage on its native tropical mudflats. Though it usually hitches along on its pectoral fins, it can also rear up on its tail and take off amazingly fast in foot-high leaps, changing direction each time it touches down.

LATERAL LINE of the southern hake is clearly visible, with conspicuous dots and a darker line running down its body from head to tail. Beneath this visible, external line is the delicate system of canals and sensory organs which, connected with the brain, enable the fish to detect currents, obstacles and even unseen enemies or prey through low-frequency vibrations.

The Mysterious Lateral Line

Any home fish tank or big-city aquarium offers practical and striking proof of the unique sixth sense possessed by fishes: the lateral line sensory system which steers them unerringly away from the invisible glass walls. Outwardly visible to a greater or lesser degree in all fishes as a line extending along each side of the body to the tail, these sensory organs function in an intermediate area between hearing and touch. Long a subject of scientific debate, it is now established that they are sensitive to low-frequency vibrations and pressure waves built up as the fish passes rocks and other barriers, or sent out by waves and currents, or by movements of solid objects under water. This is the system that enables fishes to locate unseen prey, or to sense unseen enemies and scurry to safety in the opposite direction. This is the means by which entire schools containing thousands of fish turn and maneuver as one—with every fish keeping station on its companions.

NORMAL REACTION of fish to prodding finger in their tank, as demonstrated by Dr. Theodore Walker of Scripps Institution of Oceanography, is to scurry away, warned by lateral line.

56

ABNORMAL REACTION of hooded fish in "bathing cap" studies is clearly evident as the prodding finger leaves them undisturbed. Capped by latex hoods which blocked the lateral line system of the head, the fish swam awkwardly and seemed unable to detect the approach of foreign objects. They even allowed themselves to be touched and pushed around at will.

3

The Shaping Hand of Evolution

Six hundred million years ago, when the fossil record of life on earth first begins to tell its story in some detail, this planet was already about four billion years old. Looking back down such an immensity of time, the mechanism of evolution can be visualized: as in a slow-speed movie of a flower's growth from seedling to full bloom, we can picture for ourselves the growth of life from a single-celled microorganism drifting in the sea to the complex structure of a fish we know today. For time was the key factor in the process of evolution—time for life to grow, branch out, explore, adapt itself, to develop new forms and modifications, discarding some, refining others—and time there was aplenty. If, in creating the movie of a flower's growth, a single exposure were made every week, in similarly re-creating the evolution of the fishes, one picture might have been exposed every 100,000 years to show the small but significant changes which nature made in the slow process of natural selection as the ages crept by.

Six hundred million years ago this process was confined almost entirely to the sea. Except for a few tidal algae, the land was bare, and the surrounding oceans were far different from the submarine world we know today. They were wide, warm and shallow, and all the life that they contained was on or near the

STEPS IN FISH EVOLUTION

OSTRACODERM

This early type lived 400 million years ago. It had no jaws, a bony skull and an armored back. Its spinal cord continued to the end of its tail and it had only one pair of rudimentary fins. It moved slowly, grubbing food on the muddy bottom.

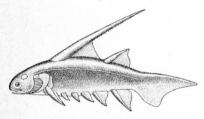

ACANTHODIAN

At this time, besides a movable jaw, the main innovation was the development of controllable and therefore more useful fins. Though this fish's fins consisted of mere spines attached to its body by folds of tissue, they helped to give it stability.

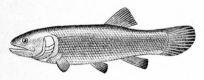

HOLOSTEAN

Flourishing 200 to 100 million years ago, this group had larger, stronger and more forward-jutting jaws. The jaw mechanism of the Holosteans distinguishes them from earlier fishes. By Cretaceous times, they were replaced by teleosts.

TELEOST

Most living bony fishes, like the yellow perch (above), are teleosts. Their jaws jut still farther forward, their fins, better placed, are more efficient. The tail fin is now symmetrical and, working with the paired fins, balances, steers and propels.

bottom. There were no fishes as we know them, but trilobites, sponges, snails, jellyfishes, worms and other creatures teemed in the waters. And somewhere, either in the oceans or in some fresh-water pond or stream of that far-off Cambrian period, was a creature that would eventually give rise to the fishes and, through them, to the amphibians, reptiles, mammals and, finally, man.

What this creature looked like, how it functioned and lived, we can only surmise, for any fossil record it might have left behind disappeared long ago, crumbled and eroded away. Many theories have been advanced for its origin. Some held that it evolved from some form of segmented worm, others that it developed from an arthropod, a phylum that includes spiders, insects and crustaceans. Most likely, however, on the basis of biochemical and structural evidence, is the hypothesis that this ancestral creature arose from a form similar to the larva of an echinoderm, which is related to the starfishes and sea urchins that we know today.

Certainly it did not look much like a fish. It probably had no paired fins, no real head, brain or advanced sense organs, jaws or teeth. Most likely, its body was cylindrical, with simple digestive organs, a nerve cord running its length from front to back, and below that a sort of stiffening, supporting rod which was its only skeleton, made of a soft material surrounded by a tough sheath. This forerunner of a backbone, or vertebral column, is called a notochord and from it the animals that possessed it, including all the vertebrates, derived their name—the chordates.

THE first chordate, as nearly as we can reconstruct it today, appears to have breathed and fed through internal gills while wriggling through the shallows. It was probably similar in appearance and mode of living to the sea lancelet, a tiny, primitive animal of modern times which lives in shallow coastal waters. But the comparison cannot be carried far, for the sea lancelet, primitive though it is, is already too specialized to be considered a truly ancestral type.

How this earliest chordate stock evolved, what stages of development it went through to eventually give rise to truly fishlike creatures, we do not know. Between the Cambrian when it probably originated, and the Ordovician when the first animals with really fishlike characteristics appeared, there is a gap of perhaps 100 million years which we have not been able to fill. But in the 45 million years which followed, up to the Devonian when fishes underwent a veritable explosion in population and species, some very significant events took place that shaped their future for all time.

The first of these was the development of jaws. Before this happened, the fishlike creatures populating the fresh water of those times were jawless, living on the bottom, sucking in mud to filter out their food through gills which served the dual purposes of feeding and breathing. These ostracoderms, as they are called for the shell-like, bony armor with which most of them were covered, became highly diversified and specialized, growing up to several feet in length. From our point of view they were grotesque creatures, hulking caricatures with few of the external features which we associate with fishes today other than the scaly hind part of their body and their odd-looking fins and tail. The descendants they bequeathed to modern times are rather grotesque too—the hagfish and lamprey, both jawless parasites which, while they look quite different, go back in a direct line to those ostracoderms of long ago.

The process of evolution is not an orderly one which goes from A to B to C; rather, significant changes may occur in one species while another species remains relatively unchanged. The ostracoderms survived for some 100 million years before they died out at the end of the Devonian. Long before that happened, however, the first fishes with jaws appeared, and this was a development no less significant than the much later one of walking limbs in the amphibians. For jaws freed those early fishes from the prison of the bottom and opened up the full, wide range of their watery world. Jaws enabled them to handle their food in bigger pieces—they could pursue and seize prey or bite off plants or even crush hard-shelled morsels like mollusks and crustaceans.

True jaws in fishes were evolved from the front gill arches. The oldest of all jawed vertebrates are the placoderms (named for their platelike body armor). Although they had only a primitive and clumsy jaw, they went a long way with it. These archaic fishes, with their head and trunk encased in a full set of armor, proliferated in the Devonian, again a time of wide, shallow seas, and before its 60 million years had passed, the placoderms had adapted their jaws to all manner of foods, developing sharp teeth for seizing and tearing, paved jaws for crushing; and some of them also showed the second significant development in the evolution of fishes—paired fins.

By this time the underwater picture had already significantly changed from the distant days of the Cambrian period. The seas had advanced and receded from the continental land masses several times. Mountain ranges had arisen and eroded, deserts had formed and been drowned. Land plants had appeared and were by now prolific, from small leafless plants a few inches high to giant tree ferns 40 feet tall. In the sea, corals flourished, building reefs where sea lilies waved in the currents and strange cephalopods crawled in their big, straight or curled shells. Mollusks were numerous and diversified, and sponges were abundant in many new forms. But the biggest change in scene from the Cambrian was in the water itself, above the bottom, where fishes of many shapes swam, populating a world that had so long been virtually empty. And the fossil record they left behind in the extensive sandstone, shale and limestone deposits of this Age of Fishes, as the Devonian is sometimes called, is profuse in its examples of how they adapted themselves to the many opportunities afforded them to spread out and to invade every niche of their environment.

THE evolution of fishes, in its simplest terms, is really a history of constant adaptation to new possibilities, specialization for different modes of living, and refinement of both of these. Such useful additions to their basic structure as they did develop, like jaws and paired fins, were in the nature of new tools to better exploit their environment and habitat, and of this the paired fins are a prime example.

When fishes started swimming actively, rather than wriggling spasmodically through the water like tadpoles, some sort of stabilizing mechanism became an urgent necessity to prevent an uncontrollable pitching and rolling. Paired fins, the pectorals and pelvics thrusting out from the sides of the body, were the answer and their development is closely associated with a greatly improved swimming skill.

When and how the paired fins originated is a matter of debate—the fossil record provides no clear answer. One theory, now largely discounted, held that they originally formed as extensions and elaborations of the gill flaps. Another explanation is that they originally evolved from longitudinal skin folds down both sides of the trunk. During that stage they were mainly for stabilizing purposes. Eventually the subdivision of these folds resulted in the differentiation into pectoral and pelvic fins. Still later, when these paired fins developed narrow bases, they became effective means of steering.

The answer now is believed by some to be found in minnow-sized predator fishes which swam side by side in Devonian waters with the placoderms. Looking somewhat like miniature sharks, these acanthodians, as they are known, are sometimes inappropriately called "spiny sharks." They had stiff spines in the pectoral and pelvic areas, as well as others elsewhere, attached to which were webs of skin supported, in some cases, by radiating bars. These alone would have been enough to give the acanthodians considerable stability in the water, and they may have had the potential of later developing into fins that were more movable and controllable. Thus it appears likely that paired fins first developed from folds of skin alongside the body—and, as they were refined still further in the fishes that followed, the paired fins became more and more maneuverable.

The acanthodians are useful fish to the paleontologist in still another way: their fossil remains also tell something of the development of jaws. From them it would appear that jaws evolved from the gill arches; and once the necessary structure and muscles had developed, jaws became increasingly versatile and specialized for their purpose, just as the paired fins grew into highly sensitive tools for steering and braking.

Fully as important in the successful evolution of fishes as their development of jaws and paired fins was their ability to adapt their basic supporting structure, whether it was outside armor or internal skeleton, to the changing possibilities offered by their environment. From the early, clumsy ostracoderms weighted down by massive armor to such swift and maneuverable fishes as the pike and the mackerel is a long, long road—and along every part of it the fishes, according to one theory, divested themselves increasingly of heavy, bony parts. Armored plates gave way to platelike scales; these in turn grew thinner and more flexible. Skeletons grew lighter and the fishes gained agility; the heavy cranial structures of so many early fishes were pared down to skulls of manageable size. Others hold that the armored fishes were a specialized side line.

Certain fishes, during the Devonian, simplified this process of getting rid of bone by not forming it in the first place. Embryos in many animals, as is well known, develop cartilaginous parts first, then gradually replace them with bone —in the case of these early fishes, they simply stayed with the cartilage. Until fairly recently, it was thought that cartilage represented an earlier stage of evolution, that the development of bone was an advance toward a higher form, but the great advances made in this century in the delicate study of fossils have shown that bone is as ancient as cartilage. In any case, it is now clear that at some point before the Devonian fishes divided into two main classes, one of which followed what might be called the cartilage road (known as the Chondrichthyes, they include today the sharks and rays, which do not have a bone in their bodies) while the other continued to develop and refine the skeletal structure along bony lines.

The jawless lampreys and hagfish, which belong to a class of their own, the cyclostomes, are a striking example of how bone was eliminated through millions of years of evolution. The descendants of the extremely bony ostracoderms, these eely-looking fishes show today no traces of the bony external armor and heavily boned cranial skeleton that characterized their ancestors. Their scales have disappeared; their skin consists only of tough, fibrous layers. Their once heavily armored head has been reduced to a small cartilaginous

UNUSUAL MODIFICATIONS OF FINS

Not all fishes use their fins exclusively for locomotion. Some, like the benthosaurus, remora and batfish, have adapted their fins to other purposes. The benthosaurus' pelvic and caudal fins have become extremely elongated and are equipped with sensory bulbs at the tips (below). The dorsal fin of the remora (opposite) has evolved into a sucker with which it attaches itself to sharks, whales, porpoises and even boats. And the batfish, a relative of the anglerfish, has developed out of a dorsal-fin spine a kind of fishing rod.

BENTHOSAURUS

Sight is of little use to the benthosaurus, which lives at very great ocean depths where there is no light. As a substitute for vision (and perhaps other senses), the creature drags its highly sensitive fin tips along the bottom, probably seeking food.

skull and the remainder of their internal skeleton consists entirely of cartilage.

When the two main classes of fishes, the cartilaginous Chondrichthyes and the higher bony fishes known as Osteichthyes, divided and went their separate ways nobody knows for certain. Why they did so is also a matter of conjecture, but it may have been simply a matter of originating in different habitats. The sharks, for instance, may have arisen from a group that became adapted at an early date to life in the sea, while the bony fishes reigned supreme in fresh water. Later a few sharks went into fresh water themselves (a few still live there), and still later the bony fishes spread far and wide in the oceans.

In any case, the two groups represent different solutions to living in their watery environment, and of the two the bony fishes have been the more successful. The cartilage-skeletoned group began to decline in importance after some 85 million years, and today has left only a relatively few families of sharks, rays and ratfishes as its descendants. The highly diversified bony fishes, on the other hand, have been the dominant form of vertebrate life in the oceans for the last 350 million years.

The living sharks, rays and ratfishes are unique in being the only group of jawed fishes with a skeleton made entirely of cartilage. The cartilage is often stiffened and strengthened, with calcium phosphate, but it has no true bone. Nor do these cartilaginous fishes have either lungs or an air bladder, or the typical fish body armor of bony plates or scales. Instead, they are likely to be partly or completely covered with skin denticles—sharp, tiny toothlike projections —or to have protective spines in strategic places.

Some of the early shark species were enormous—up to 50 feet in length—and they must have been frightening apparitions in those long-ago seas. But not all were big: another Devonian type was only about three feet long, quite modern-looking, with a jaw structure equipped with a double hinge which kept the upper jaw from moving forward or backward when the mouth was opened or closed. Still another, intermediate shark form which flourished in the Carboniferous period following the Devonian had the same kind of jaw suspension, but the paired fins were very much refined, being narrow-based and flexible, as in the modern sharks—and these so-called hybodonts, as a consequence, were very skillful and efficient swimmers. Their descendants today are the rare and primitive Port Jackson and frilled sharks.

Modern sharks began their development in the late Jurassic, perhaps 150 million years ago, and by the Cenozoic era, the Age of Mammals, they were present in large numbers and varieties. They have changed little since. More highly developed in every way than the hybodonts, their chief difference is a jaw structure in which the upper jaw is supported by a modified gill arch and not hinged directly to the skull—a mechanism that permits the mouth to move forward when they feed. There are both free-swimming sharks and bottom dwellers, and one of them, the whale shark, is the biggest fish in the sea, reaching up to 60 feet in length.

Modern skates, and rays too, are known from the Jurassic to the present day. The one other living group possibly related to the sharks are the cartilage-skeletoned chimaeras, or ratfishes. They were probably present in the Triassic, some 200 million years ago.

The Osteichthyes, or higher bony fishes, are the dominant class in the world's waters today and the most successful fishes of all time. For purposes of classification, they are divided into two main groups characterized by fin structure

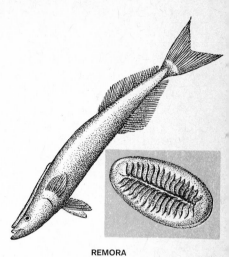

REMORA

Though the sucker of the remora is an efficient apparatus for hitching rides on large objects, it is not used for parasitic purposes. Once it has been towed to a feeding area, the remora leaves its host, searches for food and hitches another ride.

BATFISH

The bell-shaped "rod" of the batfish is a modification of the first spine of its dorsal fin, located on the forward part of its head. It is tipped with a fleshy "bait" which lures other fishes within biting range. As shown above, it is retractable.

63

FROM FISH TO FOSSIL

Three Priscacaras swim in an ancient Wyoming lake. They were a fresh-water genus abundant 50 million years ago.

A dead Priscacara falls to the bottom. Placid waters and a scarcity of scavengers allow sediments to cover the fish intact.

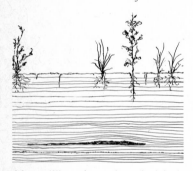

Many millions of years later the lake is gone and its bottom sediments have formed layers of shale, crushing the skeleton flat.

Still later the shale has been heaved into the air by earth movements. Erosion has set in and uncovered the fish fossil.

The fossil shows as a dark imprint of its body in the hard clay. Minerals seeping in have partly turned the bones to stone.

—those with lobed fins, in which the bony, fingerlike fin skeleton is completely enclosed in muscle to give the fin a paddlelike appearance; and those with rayed fins, the familiar fanlike structure of stiff rays connected by skin folds.

The ray-finned fishes, or actinopterygians, are more familiar today for the simple reason that there are more of them—they survived the stresses and strains of evolution better than the lobe-finned group. But if these latter are not important numerically, they are significant historically—for they include the ancestors of the first backboned animals to move onto the land.

These were the rhipidistians, fresh-water fishes that ranged worldwide for 100 million years, from the mid-Devonian almost to the end of the Paleozoic era. They were great predators, fearsome-looking with their gaping mouths, sharklike tails and large, thick scales. At some time during the late Devonian the first rhipidistians ventured forth on land. Just how or why they did this we will probably never know; only a few remains of a presumed transitional type have been found in Greenland fossil beds. Most likely, they began their adaptation to terrestrial life by moving out of ponds and streams that were slowly drying up, seeking more water, crawling over the mud with the aid of their forefins. In any case, they gave rise to the amphibians, and some of these in turn left their aquatic environment and developed into reptiles, a group that lived independently on the land and that—though there are several gaps in the fossil record—can confidently be said to have risen on the ladder of evolution to the mammals and finally man.

THE rhipidistians were extinct by the end of the Paleozoic era, possibly the victims of the very land-and-water creatures, the amphibians, to which they had given rise. Only one group of closely related survivors remained, the coelacanths, and these, as far as anyone knew until very recent times, themselves became extinct in the Cretaceous. The fact that they did not really die out, but are living today, brought about one of the strangest and most dramatic discoveries in scientific history.

At Christmastime in 1938 a trawler brought into the port of East London, in South Africa, a peculiar fish that no one had ever seen before. It had been caught at a depth of about 240 feet. Some five feet long and weighing 127 pounds, it had large, round scales, bright blue in color, and strongly lobed paired fins. Miss Courtenay Latimer, the woman curator at the East London Museum to whom the fish was first brought, recognized it as an extremely unusual specimen, and notified Professor J.L.B. Smith, a well-known ichthyologist at Rhodes University in Grahamstown. Though only the skin and part of the skull were saved, he realized it was a coelacanth and named it *Latimeria* in her honor.

For 14 years no other coelacanths were caught, but in 1952 word came to Professor Smith that another had been netted in the waters off Anjouan, an island in the French Comores, which lie between the east coast of Africa and Madagascar. Professor Smith went to Anjouan by special plane, but by the time he got there this fish, too, had largely deteriorated. Since then a dozen or more of these strange survivors of the Cretaceous have been taken from East African waters near Madagascar, and many of them have now been thoroughly studied by French and other scientists.

The coelacanths probably arose from rhipidistian stock; in any case, a close relationship between the two is indicated by such things as the structure of the brain case and the fins. But while the rhipidistians were essentially fresh-water fishes, the coelacanths have been exclusively ocean dwellers since the Jurassic.

One other group of living lobe-finned fishes remains: the dipnoans, or lungfishes. Only three forms have survived to modern times—one each in Africa, Australia and South America. Yet all trace their history back to the Devonian.

The Australian lungfish seems the closest to the early fossil types, and is generally considered the most primitive of the living species. Although it can rise to the surface to breathe, it cannot survive entirely out of water, like the lungfishes of Africa and South America, which live through the dry season buried in mud and breathing through air holes to the surface.

The early fossil lungfishes were typically fresh-water forms. They had separate dorsal, anal and caudal fins which later became fused to form a single continuous fin around one third of the body at the tail end. They also probably had lungs, though no certain traces of them have yet been found. Some forms developed eel-like bodies with long, threadlike fins.

Because the lungfishes have real lungs and the Australian form even "walks" across the mud of river and lake bottoms by using its fins like legs, it is tempting to think they might have some direct connection with the amphibians which led to the land-living vertebrates. But they do not; they are a separate group entirely, of whom it can at best be said that they are once-removed cousins of the rhipidistians, those presumably very distant ancestors of man.

As interesting and unusual as the lungfishes are, the ray-finned fishes are impressive by sheer weight of size and number. They show a truly amazing diversity of body forms and adaptations. They have developed such complex varieties that they must be considered as three large superorders. These, which represent levels of structural development and organization rather than natural similarities, are the chondrosteans, the holosteans and the teleosts.

The primitive chondrosteans had all the basic characteristics of the ray-finned fishes, but in some of them the skull and the rest of the skeleton suggest a common origin with the lobe-finned group. Their skin was covered with thick scales, diamond-shaped and somewhat overlapping; their sharklike tails were forked and powerful. A large and interesting family among these were the paleoniscids, among which were some of the most modern-looking fishes of the middle and late Devonian. Some were long and pikelike, with the fins far back; others were deep-bodied and plate-shaped. Many in this family were swift swimmers and voracious predators.

THE chondrosteans proliferated until the Jurassic, when they were replaced by more advanced forms. A few lingered into the Lower Cretaceous and left behind as their survivors some well-known descendants—the sturgeons, especially known from the Black and Caspian Seas, the curious paddlefishes of the Mississippi River and China, and the bichirs of Africa.

The holosteans, a higher category, include a number of distinct groups apparently independently derived from chondrostean ancestral stock. They show changes particularly in their swimming and feeding equipment: the fin structure is more efficient, and the jaw muscles are larger and stronger. Most of the holosteans were streamlined in a modern fashion, and their scales were thinner and more flexible. In modern fishes, this type is represented by the bowfin of the Great Lakes. But there was also a deep-bodied group, the semionotids, which had thick scales and peglike teeth—the living gar is a cousin of these. Another prominent holostean group were the pycnodonts, as round as a dish and covered with elongated scales. They had tiny mouths and crushing teeth for

TRANSITIONAL CREATURE

The lungfish (above), although classified as a fish, is a striking example of the transitional stage that early fishes may have gone through in order to become amphibians like the tiger salamander (below). Like other fishes, it has gills during both larval and adult stages and spends its life in the water. But it can survive long dry spells, estivating in the mud, has air-breathing lungs like the amphibians and uses its long, slender paired fins much the same way amphibians use their limbs.

feeding on hard-shelled invertebrates in calm reef waters. None of these survived to modern times, but their fossils are very often found in the Mesozoic rocks of Europe.

The holosteans flourished during the Jurassic, in the Age of Reptiles. It was a time of fairly equable climate when forests of pines and other conifers mingled with ginkgoes and tree ferns, and the drier slopes and plains were covered with ferns and huge, flowering cycads. The great dinosaurs dominated life on land, and in the sea giant reptiles flourished, the plesiosaurs and ichthyosaurs. By the late Cretaceous, however, they and most of the holosteans had already disappeared. The day was dawning for that very modern group of fishes known as the teleosts, which include most of the species we know today.

Although their level of development was first achieved in the Jurassic, the teleosts as a group really began to take over in the Cretaceous period, a time of extensive chalk deposits in seas in many parts of the world. The rate of their development at this time was explosive. The changes from the holostean to the teleost level, principally a matter of structural refinement, prepared these fishes for specializations enabling them to invade every part of the world of water, and especially the oceans.

In skeleton and scales the teleosts show a high degree of adaptation to efficient swimming. In speed and maneuverability they have outclassed any fishes heretofore known. Many kept the fin arrangement of the earlier actinopterygians, with the pelvics placed behind the pectorals, but by the Cretaceous there were already perchlike forms in which the pectorals had moved upward to the side of the body, and the pelvics moved forward under them. The tail changed too, with important consequences in fin placement and maneuverability—the caudal fin developed symmetrically at the end of the backbone, so that in its propulsive motion it produced no lifting action of the hind part of the body. Thus the paired fins could now be freed entirely from the necessity of counteracting the negative pitch induced by the earlier sharklike tail, and could be used efficiently for braking and tight turning.

Today the teleosts are represented by about 20,000 species of modern fishes, the vast majority of all those known in the world. They have been successful in adapting themselves to just about every environment possible for a gill-breathing vertebrate. Their tremendous variety of forms ranges from the snakelike eel to the almost globular ocean sunfish, from the arrow-swift barracuda to the strange little sea horse, from anglerfishes, porcupinefishes and sea robins to the familiar salmon, perches and trout.

The teleosts show, perhaps better than any other fishes, how the history of evolution is essentially the story of faunal succession through time. Old groups that cannot adapt themselves to change die out, and new ones take their place. Entire groups of fishes, like the ostracoderms and the placoderms, have become extinct, but others have left descendants, sometimes little changed, sometimes degenerate or greatly modified. The living coelacanth, the lungfishes, the bichir, sturgeons and hagfishes are all excellent examples of fishes that have retained the essential characteristics of their remote ancestors, however much modified, and they are found side by side with the far more advanced teleosts. Yet like the teleosts, they too are specialized and adapted to the niches they occupy. If they were not, they would not have survived the intense competition for living space. They would have died out long ago and be known to us, like their ancestors, only as fossils, mute imprints in the rocks of long ago.

A PAGE IN ROCK OF EVOLUTION'S LONG STORY, THESE FOSSIL REMAINS OF SMALL HERRINGLIKE FISH DATE BACK AT LEAST 50 MILLION YEARS

The Ascent of Fishes

Beginning as mud-sucking, armored creatures that wriggled like tadpoles across the bottom of the ancient waters, fishes slowly evolved jaws and paired fins, which in some cases now function as legs and even wings, to become the most versatile animals of their environment. Today, existing alongside the modern species, there are holdovers from the past—fishes that are living fossils.

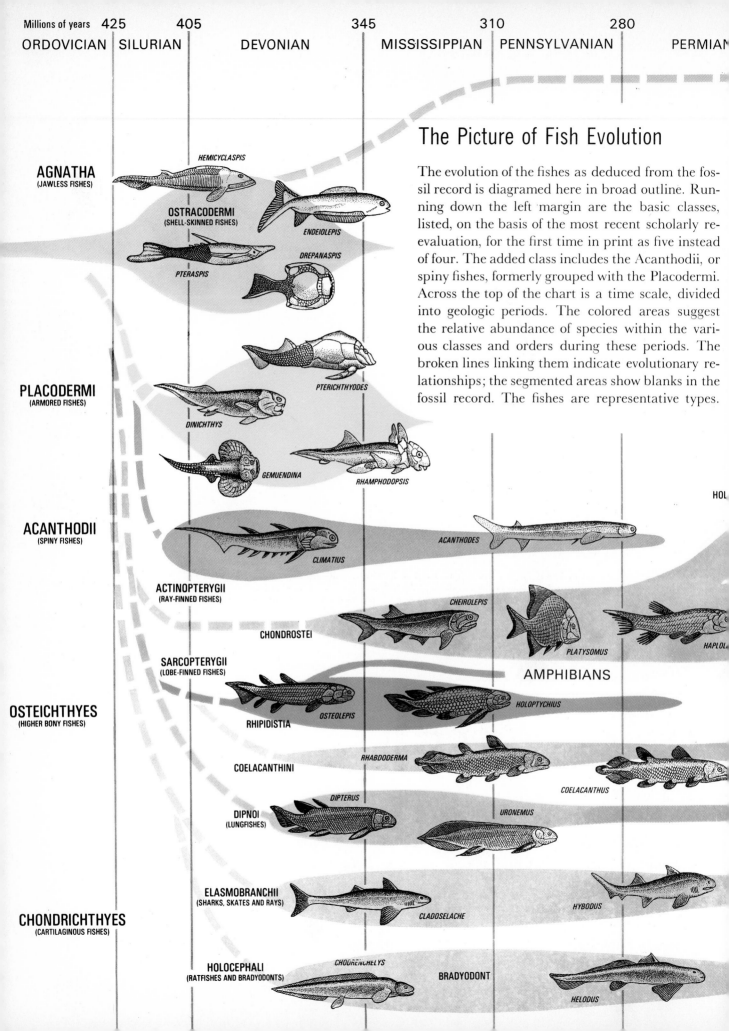

Millions of years	425		405		345		310		280	
	ORDOVICIAN	SILURIAN		DEVONIAN		MISSISSIPPIAN		PENNSYLVANIAN		PERMIAN

The Picture of Fish Evolution

The evolution of the fishes as deduced from the fossil record is diagramed here in broad outline. Running down the left margin are the basic classes, listed, on the basis of the most recent scholarly re-evaluation, for the first time in print as five instead of four. The added class includes the Acanthodii, or spiny fishes, formerly grouped with the Placodermi. Across the top of the chart is a time scale, divided into geologic periods. The colored areas suggest the relative abundance of species within the various classes and orders during these periods. The broken lines linking them indicate evolutionary relationships; the segmented areas show blanks in the fossil record. The fishes are representative types.

AGNATHA (JAWLESS FISHES)

HEMICYCLASPIS

OSTRACODERMI (SHELL-SKINNED FISHES)

ENDEIOLEPIS

PTERASPIS

DREPANASPIS

PLACODERMI (ARMORED FISHES)

PTERICHTHYODES

DINICHTHYS

GEMUENDINA

RHAMPHODOPSIS

HOL

ACANTHODII (SPINY FISHES)

CLIMATIUS

ACANTHODES

ACTINOPTERYGII (RAY-FINNED FISHES)

CHEIROLEPIS

CHONDROSTEI

PLATYSOMUS

HAPLOL

SARCOPTERYGII (LOBE-FINNED FISHES)

AMPHIBIANS

OSTEICHTHYES (HIGHER BONY FISHES)

OSTEOLEPIS

HOLOPTYCHIUS

RHIPIDISTIA

COELACANTHINI

RHABDODERMA

COELACANTHUS

DIPNOI (LUNGFISHES)

DIPTERUS

URONEMUS

ELASMOBRANCHII (SHARKS, SKATES AND RAYS)

CLADOSELACHE

HYBODUS

CHONDRICHTHYES (CARTILAGINOUS FISHES)

HOLOCEPHALI (RATFISHES AND BRADYODONTS)

CHONDRENCHELYS

BRADYODONT

HELODUS

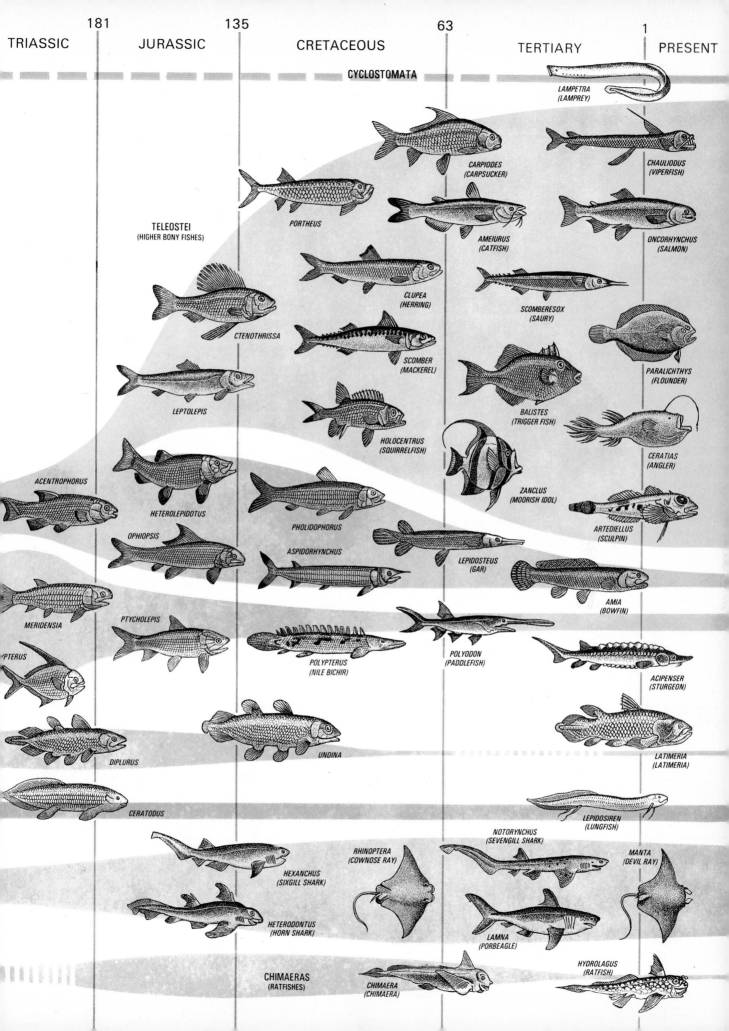

TRIASSIC   181   JURASSIC   135   CRETACEOUS   63   TERTIARY   1   PRESENT

CYCLOSTOMATA

LAMPETRA
(LAMPREY)

CARPIODES
(CARPSUCKER)

CHAULIODUS
(VIPERFISH)

PORTHEUS

TELEOSTEI
(HIGHER BONY FISHES)

AMEIURUS
(CATFISH)

ONCORHYNCHUS
(SALMON)

CTENOTHRISSA

CLUPEA
(HERRING)

SCOMBERESOX
(SAURY)

LEPTOLEPIS

SCOMBER
(MACKEREL)

PARALICHTHYS
(FLOUNDER)

BALISTES
(TRIGGER FISH)

HOLOCENTRUS
(SQUIRRELFISH)

CERATIAS
(ANGLER)

ACENTROPHORUS

HETEROLEPIDOTUS

ZANCLUS
(MOORISH IDOL)

OPHIOPSIS

PHOLIDOPHORUS

ARTEDIELLUS
(SCULPIN)

ASPIDORHYNCHUS

LEPIDOSTEUS
(GAR)

MERIDENSIA

AMIA
(BOWFIN)

PTYCHOLEPIS

POLYPTERUS
(NILE BICHIR)

POLYODON
(PADDLEFISH)

...PTERUS

ACIPENSER
(STURGEON)

DIPLURUS

UNDINA

LATIMERIA
(LATIMERIA)

CERATODUS

NOTORYNCHUS
(SEVENGILL SHARK)

LEPIDOSIREN
(LUNGFISH)

HEXANCHUS
(SIXGILL SHARK)

RHINOPTERA
(COWNOSE RAY)

MANTA
(DEVIL RAY)

HETERODONTUS
(HORN SHARK)

LAMNA
(PORBEAGLE)

HYDROLAGUS
(RATFISH)

CHIMAERAS
(RATFISHES)

CHIMAERA
(CHIMAERA)

PREHISTORIC HOLDOVER, the Australian lungfish has a fish-like body, flipperlike fins and, unlike the African and South American species, large scales and only one lung. It is unable to survive out of water in a dry mud ball or tunnel as its cousins can, but tolerates foul or stagnant pools, occasionally rising to the surface for air. Generally docile, it fights wildly in a net.

AN AFRICAN LUNGFISH IS CHIPPED FREE OF A BALL OF BAKED MUD

Fishes with Lungs

Lungfishes belong to the ancient order of the dipnoans—fishes with both gills and lungs. They date back 390 million years, to the middle of the Devonian, when ponds and streams began to dry up and many fishes died. The lungfishes were not only able to breathe air but to travel from mud puddle to mud puddle on paddlelike fins. Eventually they acquired the ability to lie dormant in the mud, where they waited for the seasonal rains. Today the lungfishes demonstrate their continuing tenacity by surviving, in some cases, up to four years out of water.

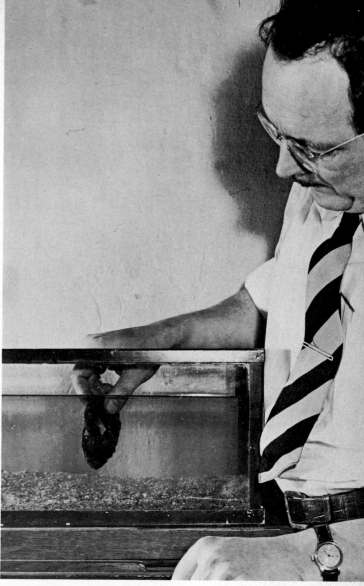

FREED FROM THE MUD, the lungfish remains in a stiffly curled position as it is dropped into a tank of water. During encystment it must lie with its tail over its eyes to prevent loss of moisture.

GETTING THE KINKS OUT, 12 hours after immersion, the lungfish soaks on the bottom of the tank. It still wears remnants of the leathery cocoon which it secreted almost completely around itself in the drying mud. While estivating it lived off its muscle tissue—hence its desiccated look—and stored its waste products after filtering out and recirculating the precious water.

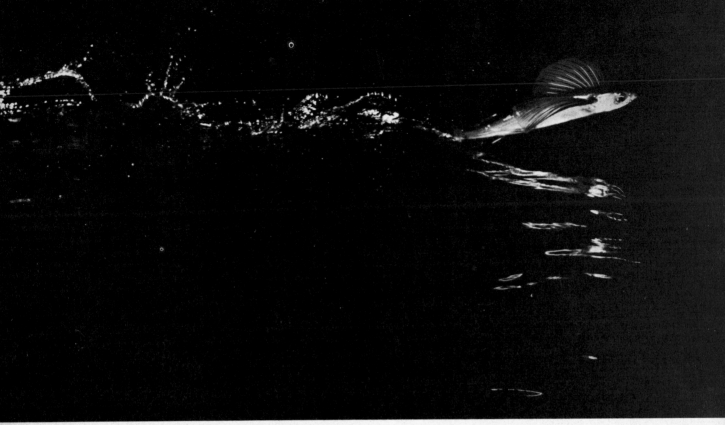

A FLYINGFISH leaves the water with outstretched pectoral fins which, held rigid, will serve as wings during a prolonged, 35-mile-an-hour glide. Prior to flight, the tail served as a miniature outboard motor, beating back and forth as much as 50 times a second and helping lift the fish into the air. Flyingfishes use their aerial skills as a way of escaping from their enemies.

Different Adaptations for Different Environments

Evolution has equipped the fishes shown on these pages with odd adaptations or behavior patterns for getting along in or out of their environments. Eels, which begin life in one environment, salt water, must journey 2,000 to 5,000 miles to another, fresh water, to mature. But when young, they are weak swimmers, and thus they ride toward their destination on ocean currents. Flyingfishes escape their environment briefly to avoid predators, sometimes soaring as high as 15 or 20 feet on fins with a wingspread of six to 20 inches. Mudskippers leave theirs entirely. Dwelling in the shallow, brackish coastal

A POP-EYED MUDSKIPPER DEMONSTRATES ITS POWERS OF LOCOMOTION ON A CARDBOARD RAMP. BALANCING ON ITS PELVIC FINS, IT DRAWS ITSEL

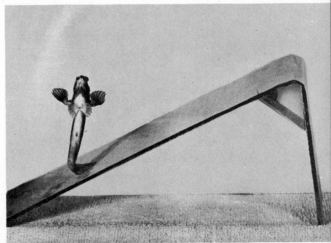

A EUROPEAN EEL glides through the weeds of a shallow pond. Eels take up to three years to migrate from their spawning grounds; upon entering streams, they clamber over obstructions in pursuit of still waters and muddy bottoms. They do not travel overland as believed; their presence in isolated ponds is attributed to their ability to go through underground waterways.

waters of Africa, Asia and Australia, they flip-flop ashore in search of insects and edge forward, a half inch at a time, doing a little over two miles an hour, on their strong pectoral fins. They suggest, in this ability, the ancient, air-breathing, lobe-finned fishes that gave rise to the amphibians. Sometimes they use their tails for thrust and take-off in yard-long leaps. Though lungless, mudskippers can stay out of water for prolonged periods because they carry water around with them. A supply stored in spongy sacs keeps their gills wet—and thus permits normal "underwater" respiration to continue on land.

RWARD WITH ITS WELL-MUSCLED, LIMBLIKE PECTORAL FINS, THEN REARS UP ON ITS TAIL FOR A SOMERSAULT. REACHING THE TOP, IT FALLS OFF

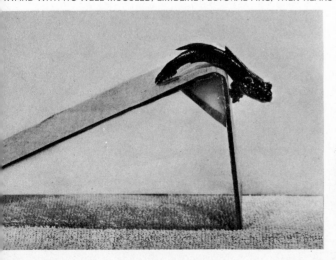

Living Fishes from the Prehistoric Past

The coelacanths, the fish that were supposed to have died out 70 million years ago, are the world's oldest living higher animals, predating the dinosaurs by almost 200 million years. Unlike the degenerate paddlefish above and the archaic long-nosed gar opposite, survivors of ancient orders, the coelacanths have undergone little change in 300 million years and thus have been described as "machines for reading the past backward." Their hearts and pituitary glands are at such an early stage of evolutionary development that scientists studying them have found startling confirmation in them of theories about the construction of these organs in early vertebrates. Because the coelacanths are related to the extinct air-breathing rhipidistians, the aquatic ancestors of all land animals, much attention has been focused on their fins in the hope that they will tell more about how fins became limbs.

THE COELACANTH IS MARKED BY THE FANLIKE TUFT AT THE END OF ITS TAIL. NO OTHER FISH HAS OR HAS EVER HAD SUCH A TAIL PATTERN. OTH

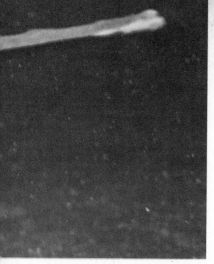

A PADDLEFISH bags its food with its enormous mouth (*above*). A relative of the first major group of ray-finned fishes, it has a cartilaginous skeleton and an almost scaleless body, unlike its heavy-scaled predecessors.

A LONG-NOSED GAR, descendant of fish that flourished 50 million years ago, still wears their ancient armor of thick, diamond-shaped scales. Burdened by this, the gar is sluggish, but moves fast when feeding.

CHARACTERISTIC COELACANTH FEATURES ARE LARGE, BLUE, ENAMELED SCALES AND LOBED FINS, ATTACHED BY "STALKS" TO THE LONG BODY

4

Sharks and Rays: Legendary Loners of the Sea

THE sharks and rays, modern members of the ancient class of Elasmobranchii, have always played a particular role in man's long association with the sea. They are the survivors of one of the most primitive groups of vertebrates —for 350 million years this branch of the fishes has pursued a lonely course down the devious road of evolution, meeting the problems of changing conditions by changing themselves. Some live at great depths in the sea, others at the surface, a few in fresh water. Some are luminous. Because of the fearsome reputation which some sharks have as killers, they inspire in man a kind of atavistic horror. To become aware of a shark approaching in dim waters from just beyond the range of vision, or of a manta ray flapping like some prehistoric monster near the ocean surface, is to experience a nightmare sense of peering down some dreadful corridor into the abysmal past when the sea held creatures even more terrible than they.

A close-up look at a large shark or ray does little to allay these nameless fears. The typical shark is one of the most beautifully streamlined of all fishes, long and graceful as it cruises through the water, torpedolike in its whiplash bursts of speed—but from head to tail it seems a creature of pure evil. Its mouth is grim and crescent-shaped, curved backward in an unchanging, savage snarl beneath its shovel-edged snout. Inside that mouth are row upon row of teeth for seizing, shearing, piercing or crunching—teeth which renew themselves at frequent intervals, as the teeth in each row grow and move forward until the front ones come into service when the row previously at the margin falls out. These teeth are actually specialized versions of the thousands of "teeth" with which the shark's entire skin is covered—tiny, razor-sharp, close-set denticles which can flay a swimmer with a single sideways swipe or lunge of the long body. The eyes, set far apart on either side of the head, are fixed as though in a cold stare. The paired forefins thrust out from behind the gill openings like the vanes of a submarine—fixed and relatively inflexible, they are used mainly for steering, for the shark is incapable of stopping short or backing up, and attacks its prey in wild, swerving lunges. The tail, its long upper lobe directly supported by the spinal column, is a powerful propulsive instrument which in one species, the thresher shark, has been particularly developed for hunting: longer than the body of the shark itself and curved like a scythe, it is used as a flail to herd together and stun large schools of fish to satisfy the thresher's voracious appetite.

RAYS and their cousins, the skates, are scarcely less sinister in appearance. They are flattened from above, and their pectoral fins have expanded and become attached to their heads, forming triangular, winglike shapes which give them the appearance of sea-borne bats. Many rays, unlike the sharks, have smooth skins, with patches of thorny or knifelike denticles in some species. In the great manta ray, or devilfish, two hornlike projections which add to its nightmarish look have grown outward on either side of its mouth, as a funnel-like aid in feeding. The tails of most rays and of all skates have thinned out to the point where they are whiplike. The sting rays carry barbs at the base of the tail with a poison so potent that it causes intense pain and can even kill a man. These, however, are the only rays that are harmful to humans—it is their appearance rather than any innate ferocity which has made these bottom-dwelling fish the creatures of dreadful legend that they are.

In addition to having skeletons made entirely of cartilage, the elasmobranchs differ in other ways from the bony fishes. Their gills are generally primitive, with separate openings. A shark simply has five to seven gill slits on each side of the body behind the head, a ray has a double row of gill slits on the underside of the body. A diminished gill opening called the spiracle is found in some sharks just behind the eye. The spiracle is more important to the skates and rays, among which it appears as a larger, round aperture on the upper surface of the body, fitted with a nonreturn valve which opens and closes as the fish breathes. Water is drawn in from above, and expelled through the gill slits.

Another feature characteristic of sharks and rays is the so-called spiral valve in the intestine. The name is somewhat misleading—actually, the spiral valve is a device to increase the absorptive surface of the intestines, which are much shorter than those of most vertebrates (a 10-foot shark, for example, has only nine feet of intestines, by comparison with 25 feet in a six-foot man). Though it varies in shape in different species, the spiral valve is built generally on the principle of a circular ramp or, when more tightly coiled, a series of spiraling scrolls one inside the other, with the food passing through the spirals in the process of digestion. Since it may have as many as 45 turns, the absorptive surface provided within a rather limited space is quite impressive.

Neither sharks nor rays have gas bladders, a fact of less significance to the

A SHARK'S TEETH

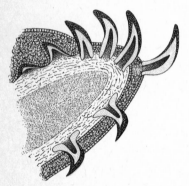

The sharp scales that cover a shark's body also extend inside its jaw, where they serve as teeth. In this sectional view of the tip of a shark's jaw, the two pointed objects at the bottom are scales, their size greatly exaggerated to show the shape of their roots, which hold them permanently in place. All the others are teeth. Unlike the teeth of most vertebrates, which are anchored to a jawbone, those of a shark grow in its skin, moving steadily forward as they increase in size, their roots emerging on the skin surface at last, when the teeth fall out as they are worn with age.

largely bottom-dwelling rays than to the foraging sharks, which literally must swim or sink. Some species overcome this lack in a makeshift sort of way by gulping air into their stomachs. Occasionally, when captured or seeking deeper water, they expel the trapped air forcefully in a prolonged belch—an action that may be the basis for ancient accounts of the roaring of sharks. Certain small and little-known shark species that live in mid-depth far out in the ocean have also developed oversized livers with comparatively huge quantities of hydrocarbon oils. Functioning on the same principle as the gasoline-filled tank which provides buoyancy in the ascent and descent of a bathysphere on its deep-sea explorations, the lighter-than-water liver oils serve to keep these sharks at their desired depths.

An outstanding feature of the sharks is their extraordinary sense of smell. A proportionately large share of the shark's brain is given over to the function of smelling. The forward part has two forks extending toward the nostrils on either side of the snout, and their perception is so delicate that the shark can actually steer itself up a scent trail much as an airplane follows a radio beam. Thus, when it first picks up a trace, it may veer back and forth, establishing the direction from which the scent comes: if the scent grows weaker on the right side, it turns back to the left; if the trail grows weaker on the left, it turns right, until at last the shark is zeroed-in and follows the scent toward its source, often a quarter of a mile or more away. Experiments have shown that if one nostril is plugged up, the shark will swim in circles, following the scent that it receives from one side only.

The sense of sight among elasmobranchs is far less acute, though they are probably not so nearsighted as they were long popularly believed to be. Whether or not they see in color is at present a matter of scientific controversy; while it was once thought that several species could distinguish one color from another, recent experiments to prove this capability have all been negative.

LIKE most fishes, elasmobranchs probably hear little. Their ears are mainly balance organs, containing the semicircular canals which inform the fish of changes in direction, acceleration or deceleration and whether it is right side up in the water. There are no main channels to the outside of the head, however, nor is there an eardrum for detecting sound waves.

Concentrated on the heads and faces of both sharks and rays are small sense organs sunk at the bottom of pits, each with a minute pore to the outside of the skin, which transmit vibrations and changes in the flow of water. Corresponding to the lateral-line organs in the higher bony fishes, these continue along a line back to the tail in a fine tube beneath the skin, which opens at intervals to the outside through minute canals. On the head, these organs are supplemented by what are called the ampullae of Lorenzini, very deep canals filled with a jellylike substance which are sensitive to electrical stimuli and changes in temperature and water pressure.

In their breeding habits sharks, skates and rays are in a class by themselves, more advanced and highly organized than most higher fishes. The two sexes copulate, the egg is fertilized inside the female, and in many species the young are born alive. In the male, a pair of projecting rods, formed from the inner parts of the pelvic fins, are the instruments of fertilization. Grooved on their inner faces and stiffened with cartilage, these claspers, as they are still called, actually do not clasp as they were once thought to, but act as dilaters to direct the sperm into the female opening. They are brought forward, erected and thrust into the

PURSES FOR EGGS

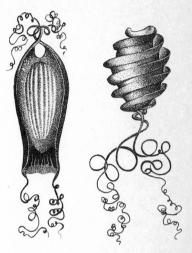

CAT SHARK   **PORT JACKSON SHARK**

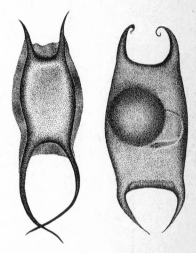

SKATE   **EMBRYO IN CASE**

CHIMAERA

The empty leathery "mermaids' purses" which wash up on sea beaches are actually egg cases of skates and sometimes sharks. Those of some species, like the cat shark and the Port Jackson shark, have long tendrils which catch in seaweed, keeping the case in place while the embryo develops. Skate egg cases have pointed "horns" at each end and their sticky undersides adhere to stones, sand and weeds. Each case contains a single embryo which takes up to 15 months to develop, depending on the species. The egg case of the chimaeras, or ratfishes, is spindle-shaped. A long tail anchors it in the sandy bottom.

female, the grooves along their inner faces forming a tube through which the sperm flows.

The eggs are large and plentifully supplied with yolk. Skates and cat sharks eject the fertilized eggs one or two at a time in flattened, cushion-shaped capsules which are formed around the egg as it passes down the oviduct. The shells of the capsules harden in the water to form the leathery "mermaids' purses" which so often are found in seaweed along the high-tide mark. Each purse has a short, hollow horn at each corner, through which sea water can freely pass to aerate the eggs. The young fish, after several months, emerges from the purse as a miniature replica of its parents. The common nurse shark and some of its relatives, on the other hand, produce similar eggs in horny shells, but retain them within the oviducts of the mother until hatching takes place.

Most sharks and rays that live in the open sea are live-bearers and produce their young fully formed. The embryo develops inside the oviduct, feeding on its very large yolk sac. In addition, many have ways of supplementing the nourishment of the developing young. One such is a form of milk supplied from the oviduct walls of rays. In some sharks, a placentalike structure develops from which the embryo is fed through a tube similar to an umbilical cord.

In most sharks and rays breeding takes place on a seasonal basis, and some of the larger sharks bear young only in alternate years. The smaller sharks, as a rule, bear only a few at a time. The common white-tipped and black-tipped sharks of Indo-Pacific waters may have up to four or six, but rarely more. The big scavengers, like the tiger or the hammerhead, often carry as many as 20 or more young at a time.

ALL sharks are carnivores, but the largest species, the basking shark and the whale shark, live on the smallest form of animal food in the sea, the zooplankton. Most of the big sharks are primarily fish eaters, but sea birds, turtles, small porpoises and even terrestrial animals, including man, are part of their diet. Rays, except for the biggest ones, the mantas, which are also plankton eaters, feed on fishes, mollusks, crustaceans, sea urchins and other creatures that live on the bottom. Unlike some of the sharks, they are not aggressive in their feeding habits, and even the biggest will never make an unprovoked attack on man.

The popular lore of what sharks will eat is unending and mostly misleading. Certain it is that they are exceedingly voracious animals which seem to wolf their food with little regard for what it is. E. W. Gudger, of the American Museum of Natural History, found in the stomach of a tiger shark fish bones, grass, feathers, bones of marine birds, fragments of turtle shell, some old cans, a dog's

A SHARK CATALOGUE

Sharks range throughout the world's seas. They are most numerous at the equator, rare near the poles, and vary enormously in size and habits. Of the seven representative species drawn to scale here, the basking shark is the largest. It is a harmless plankton feeder and may exceed 40 feet in length. The white shark, a rare 25-footer, is one of the swiftest, most dangerous of sharks. As a man-eater it overshadows the hammerhead, a scourge of the tropics, reaching 15 feet and weighing half a ton.

80

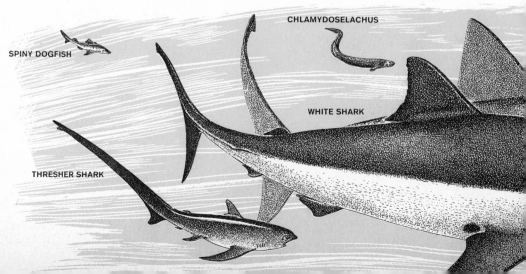

vertebrae and the skull of a cow minus the horns. In Mauritius a large shark taken in a net in Port Louis harbor had a kerosene can in its stomach. Another had a horse's head and bits of a bicycle. This appears to uphold the widespread belief that sharks are scavengers that will eat anything, but the term "scavenger" can really be applied only to the tiger shark, which *will* gulp anything. Actually, sharks are scavengers only in a secondary sense, as most carnivorous fishes are: they will attack and eat wounded or dying sea animals, but there is little real proof that they will preferentially feed on carrion.

Because sharks' mouths are far back on the underside of their heads, it is commonly believed that they must turn on their backs to seize their food. In actual fact, they generally lunge at it from below. Perry W. Gilbert, who has been studying sharks at the Lerner Marine Laboratory of the American Museum of Natural History at Bimini in the Bahamas, has described how a shark, when attacking a large fish, such as a 400-pound marlin hanging on a hook, brakes with its pectoral fins and then points upward slightly as its mouth seizes the bait. "It opens its jaws wide, the lower jaw dropping downward and the upper jaw protruding markedly from beneath the thin upper lip. . . . Then it closes its jaws and shakes the entire forward part of its body violently from side to side until it has torn 10 to 15 pounds of tissue from the marlin."

Sharks have always been considered fierce and aggressive animals, but whether this is truly so is debatable. Their behavior varies greatly. They may come up in dozens from the dark depths to inspect a piece of bait, then spend a long time circling it before one of them makes a lunge. If, while this cautious investigation is going on, the bait is given a sudden jerk, they may scatter as if in fright, and it will be a minute or two before they begin their cautious circling once again.

Blood in the water, however, has a maddening effect on them. A kind of wild fury, called the "feeding frenzy," overtakes the sharks and they charge in regardless of all risk and against all opposition. If one of their number is wounded they even turn on their own kind, attacking instantly and with great ferocity.

Several species of shark attack man, though why and under what circumstances is far from certain. Skin divers have had face-to-face encounters with sharks and escaped unhurt; they have also been attacked with no provocation. Wherever sharks abound horrible fatalities occur from time to time, and in particularly shark-infested areas, such as some Australian beaches, shark fences and patrols are an absolute necessity to protect bathers. The Shark Research Panel of the American Institute of Biological Sciences now keeps a Shark At-

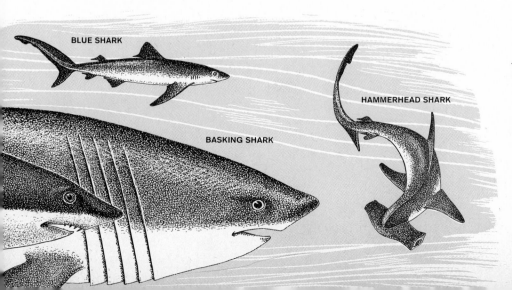

BLUE SHARK

BASKING SHARK

HAMMERHEAD SHARK

The 18-foot thresher, a tropical species, is believed to use its scythelike tail to herd and stun smaller fishes. The 12-foot blue shark of tropical and warm temperate waters is probably the most numerous of all sharks. The five-foot frilled shark, or Chlamydoselachus, a species found in the Pacific and off southern Europe, is shaped like an eel and is no menace to man. The most familiar shark to Americans is the harmless spiny dogfish that roams temperate seas all over the world.

THE SKATES AND RAYS

This is a large family of shark-related fishes that usually lie half buried in mud or sand, and have become flattened from the top into the various kite and banjo shapes shown here. Their mouths are on their undersides and are adapted for grubbing for shellfish and other small bottom dwellers. Some, like the torpedo, generate electric charges. The sting ray has a poisonous tail barb. The big sawfish digs with its toothed blade, and uses it as a flail against small fishes. The skates are harmless to man. Some of them reach seven feet in diameter and are excellent eating. Although it looks and acts like a ray, the angel shark is actually a true shark.

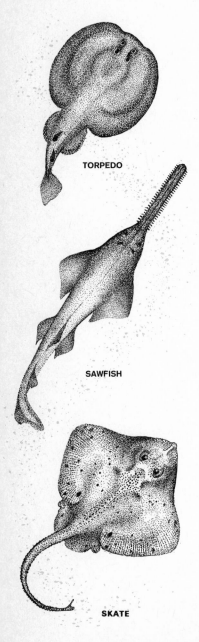

TORPEDO

SAWFISH

SKATE

tack File. It lists shark attacks in all parts of the world, starting with the report of a Portuguese seaman's death in 1580. More than 1,500 case histories are on file, of which roughly half deal with fatal attacks. Each year from 50 to 100 new cases are recorded. The attacks occur mostly in tropical seas, off the Australian and North American coasts, and in Pacific waters. But they have happened in temperate seas and even rivers as well. One unexpected incident took place a full 150 miles upstream in the Limpopo River in southern Africa; according to the file "one canoe was bitten in two and turned over and its occupants forced to swim to shore, and a dinghy with two occupants was used as a toy by a school of sharks which swirled around and around."

WHY sharks attack human beings has never been adequately answered. It has generally been assumed that the motive is hunger. Human victims have often been partially or entirely eaten by sharks, and occasionally the stomach of a captured shark is found to contain human remains. Yet sharks are by nature fish eaters, not regular consumers of human flesh. Mounting evidence compiled by researchers during the past decade suggests that the feeding drive in attacks on humans may not be as significant as hitherto believed. In many cases wounds from shark attacks appear to be lacerations from the shark's rough, denticle-studded skin or fins, or from the openmouthed use of the teeth as a sort of ripsaw. Such wounds do not indicate attempts to feed on the victims, but suggest instead that sharks are driven to attack by some aggressive urge.

Because of uncertainty about the cause of shark attacks, antishark measures have so far not been too successful. The most effective, and expensive, way to protect portions of popular swimming beaches is with fences or a maze of gill nets, as is done in Australia and South Africa. Curtains of air bubbles rising from perforated hoses and electrical barriers that jolt the sharks have also been tried. Such barriers keep some sharks away, but others nonchalantly swim through.

Still more difficult is the protection of an individual in shark-infested waters. Shark repellents have a long history of failure. Mediterranean sailors in the early 18th Century believed that casting bread upon the waters would forestall attacks—the only noticeable effect was to create hungry sailors. A chemical repellent that stains the area around a swimmer with a dye may turn away some species of shark, but it does not always work. More than 200 chemicals aimed at poisoning or incapacitating sharks have proved unsatisfactory when tested on different species of dangerous shark under various conditions. A very effective device—more of a camouflage than a repellent—has been designed to protect survivors of air and sea disasters: the shark screen. It is a thin, strong plastic one-man bag topped by three brightly colored, inflatable rings. The survivor simply stays in the water-filled bag, which floats in the ocean. The dark underside of the bag conceals any movement or bleeding, both powerful stimulants to sharks.

For the hapless individual who finds himself in shark-inhabited waters with no such equipment, the best course is to avoid giving any stimulus, olfactory, auditory or visual, to the sharks. Thrashing usually invites an attack. Some people have survived by merely playing dead. Others, in desperation, have scared sharks away by shouting, kicking the shark's head or chasing it aggressively. Such actions are a pure gamble, since their effectiveness depends on the species of shark encountered, not to mention the mood of a particular shark.

Some 35 out of 250 species of living sharks are known to attack man. The most formidable is the great white shark, or man-eater, of wide distribution. The biggest one on record was 36 1/2 feet long; the average size of the mature male is around 14 feet, with 16 feet not uncommon. The hammerhead is also feared. It is mainly a shallow-water shark, whose eyes and nostrils are carried out on wings on either side of the head, giving the creature a more than usually sinister appearance. What exactly is the use of this curious shape is not known. It may give a wider range of vision and scent, or it may give greater maneuverability.

The lemon and tiger sharks, the mako and Australian whaler (not to be confused with the whale shark) have all been accused of attacking man from time to time. The lemon and whaler hug the shore, lurking around estuaries. The others are rovers of the open sea, only coming inshore from time to time in pursuit of the fishes they normally feed on. Two more dangerous sharks are the white-tip and bull sharks. Considered one of the most vicious types off Florida and South Africa, the bull shark has also been found ascending the San Juan River to Lake Nicaragua.

The largest sharks of all are, curiously enough, the only truly harmless ones. The temperate basking shark and the tropical whale shark stick to their diet of plankton, small fishes, squids and shrimps, and are not only inoffensive but downright mild of temper.

The basking shark of north temperate waters may reach a length of 45 feet and the whale shark, its tropical counterpart, a length of 50 or 60 feet. Both have a great many small teeth, but their real feeding instruments are their gill rakers. They are sluggish, harmless creatures which often lie on the surface basking in the sun. The basking shark is encountered in large schools in the spring and early summer off the west coasts of the British Isles but at other times of the year it is solitary. At all times of the year it is highly unpopular with drift-net fishermen and regarded as a pest because it gets foul of their nets.

COW-NOSED RAY

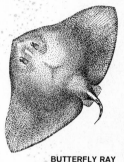

BUTTERFLY RAY

I N spite of their notoriety, sharks can also benefit mankind. Shark meat is eaten extensively in Mexico and Japan, and constitutes much of the fish 'n' chips in London and Sydney. Shark's fin has long been considered a delicacy in China. At the Mote Marine Laboratory in Sarasota, Florida, 15 scientists are using sharks in biomedical research in their study of immunology, virology and human physiology.

From the true sharks the elasmobranchs go on to more and more flattened forms, like the angel shark, a raylike shark, and the guitarfish and sawfish, sharklike rays. The huge sawfish has a long snout armed with rows of teeth on either side. Actually, these are modified skin denticles which the sawfish uses to slash its prey in the shoal waters where it lives.

Finally, there are the rays—skates, electric rays, eagle rays, mantas and the like—which live splayed out on the bottom. Some of the rays may be of enormous size—one of the Atlantic species is aptly named the barndoor skate. Sting rays may be as large as six feet across, and the great black-and-white manta ray may be 22 feet from wing tip to wing tip. The smallest rays, found in the South Seas, are five inches or less as adults.

The manta is sometimes called "devilfish" because of the two fleshy horns flanking the mouth, which is at the front end of the body, not underneath as in most rays. It uses the horns to make a funnel around the mouth when feeding on the small fishes with which it supplements its plankton diet. In addition to its nightmarish size, the manta has the extraordinary habit of throwing itself high

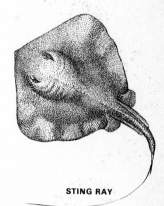

STING RAY

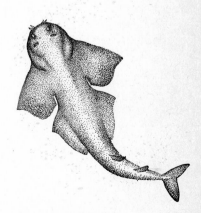

ANGEL SHARK

out of the water, landing with a noise like a cannon shot. These leaps are thought to rid the creature of fish lice, but sometimes the newborn young are shot out in mid-air, and females may leap to eject their little ones.

Sting rays are named for the daggerlike spines near the base of their tails, which are the characteristic weapons of this family of about 100 species. Each sting has a narrow groove down the side, along which runs a strip of poisonous tissue. The daggers are modified skin denticles and, just as with the shark's teeth, when one wears out another is ready to take its place. Often there are two, occasionally even three, one behind the other.

The pain of the stings is terrible and death may result from shock or heart failure. Thus even the smallest sting ray should be handled carefully. Even gloves do not guarantee protection—the sting may go right through them. The spine is doubtless a protective device, though not always effective—sharks, for instance, have been caught with numerous ray spines broken off and embedded in the skin around their mouths.

ALL skates and some rays have small electric organs. In the skates, these are located along the sides of the tail and are supplied with nerves leading from the spinal cord. In the rays, the electric organs, capable of delivering a powerful shock, are located in the wings, or shoulders, with the nerves coming from the brain. In both types, the organs are formed from modified muscle fibers. They consist of a series of batterylike electroplaxes, or electroplates, that are actually disk-shaped cells, each of which is enclosed in a compartment of connective tissue with nerves on one side and blood vessels on the other. The blood-vessel sides of the cells are those which release the discharge. The cells are connected in series, which increases their power just as voltage is increased by hooking up storage batteries in series. The electrical current is produced by a chemical reaction beginning in the nerves. Once a shock has been released, a certain period of time is needed to allow the electric energy to build up to full charge again.

The largest and most powerful of these electric organs are those of the electric, or torpedo, rays, dwellers of shallow tropical and temperate waters. Some are very small, others reach up to five feet from wing tip to wing tip. A large torpedo ray may have as many as 1,050 electroplates linked in series on each side of its body, and shocks of 220 volts have been measured—twice the voltage of ordinary household current and more than enough to knock a man down. The discharge goes from the belly to the back, the blood-vessel side of the electroplates being on the upper side.

Just what purpose these electric organs serve is still a matter of debate among scientists. Most authorities agree, however, that they are used defensively in almost all cases and offensively on occasion, according to the fish's feeding habits. It is possible that they may be used also for identification in areas where visual recognition is difficult—setting up lines of electric force in the water around it, the fish may be able, for example at breeding time, to keep other species at a distance while seeking its mate.

In any case, it seems fitting that these members of the ancient class of the elasmobranchs should be equipped with one of the most mysterious and inexplicable weapons in the sea. It emphasizes once more the fact that these creatures, from the fiercest shark to the smallest ray flapping its harmless way along the shallow shore waters, are different from any of the other fishes, travelers down a narrow road who through the long millennia have evolved and fought for their survival in their own particular way.

ITS MOUTH RINGED WITH RAPIERLIKE TEETH, THIS FOUR-FOOT NORTH ATLANTIC SAND SHARK PROWLS CLOSE TO SHORE IN SEARCH OF FOOD

Primitive Sea Scourges

Relics of the distant past, sharks have survived 350 million years of fierce competition for food and living space. Powerful and swift, ranging up to a terrifying 50 feet in length, they are utterly unpredictable predators with an appetite for everything from plankton to people. Together with the rays and skates, sharks as a class are anatomically unique among all the diverse creatures of the sea.

The Anatomy of a Shark

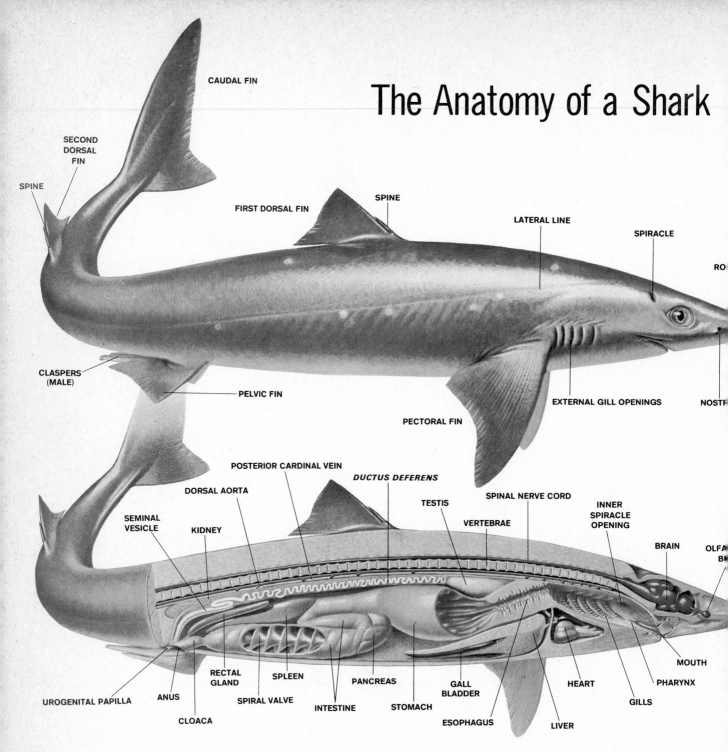

CAUDAL FIN

SECOND DORSAL FIN

SPINE

FIRST DORSAL FIN

SPINE

LATERAL LINE

SPIRACLE

RO

CLASPERS (MALE)

PELVIC FIN

EXTERNAL GILL OPENINGS

NOSTR

PECTORAL FIN

POSTERIOR CARDINAL VEIN

DUCTUS DEFERENS

DORSAL AORTA

TESTIS

SPINAL NERVE CORD

INNER SPIRACLE OPENING

SEMINAL VESICLE

KIDNEY

VERTEBRAE

BRAIN

OLFA B

UROGENITAL PAPILLA

ANUS

RECTAL GLAND

SPLEEN

SPIRAL VALVE

PANCREAS

INTESTINE

STOMACH

GALL BLADDER

ESOPHAGUS

HEART

LIVER

GILLS

MOUTH

PHARYNX

CLOACA

It Is an Odd Mixture of Ancient and Modern

The cartilaginous sharks and rays, of which the spiny dogfish above is a typical example, are both more primitive and more advanced than the bony fishes, as a comparison with the anatomical painting of the striped bass on pages 46 and 47 will show. Sharks lack bony gill covers; their gills show as a row of slits on either side of their bodies just behind their heads. Some species have a pair of openings, called the spiracles, near the eyes. The placement of fins is not so advanced as in the bony fishes, but the claspers of the pelvic fins allow the males to copulate with the females, a more up-to-date method than the wasteful external fertilization used by bony fishes. The shark has not developed a gas bladder and must keep in motion to avoid sinking. Its brain is small, but its huge smelling organ, the olfactory bulb, gives it one of the keenest noses of all fishes. The shark intestine is extremely efficient, compensating for its shortness by a spiral structure which gives maximum absorptive surface.

A GRIM-LOOKING BLUE SHARK, its wide mouth fixed in a half-moon, brakes its powerful thrust with a curve of its big pectoral fins just before lunging forward for a kill. Taken by scuba diver Peter Gimbel from a protective cage in the waters of the Atlantic Ocean off Montauk, New York, this photograph precedes the one on the following pages by only a few seconds.

A DEAD BOTTLENOSE loses a huge chunk of flesh to the blue shark shown circling warily on the previous page. Like many other large sharks, the blue first slowly swims around its victim at a distance of eight or 10 feet, then speeds up, tightening its circle as it does so. When it suddenly moves in for the first bite, little short of death can stop it from attacking. After a few large

mouthfuls the shark may race the length of its victim's body like a man chomping corn on the cob, until the prey is ripped to shreds. If a group of sharks is involved in the onslaught and one of them is accidentally injured and begins to bleed, the others will quickly turn on it, tearing their brother apart with the same relish they show in devouring an anonymous stranger.

THE LEOPARD SHARK, despite its savage appearance, is harmless and seldom exceeds six feet in length. Found in California waters, it is easily identified by its wide, alternating spots.

THE SAND TIGER, spotted when young, ranges warm, shallow Atlantic waters (*below*). Although not dangerous off the U.S., its Australian cousin, the grey nurse, is a man-eater.

THE WHALE SHARK is the largest of all fishes, sometimes reaching a length of 50 feet. As the approaching swimmer above shows, however, it is also one of the most docile, feeding mostly on plankton strained from the water by sievelike rakers on its gill arches. Gathering in schools at the sunny surface, sluggish whale sharks have been taken unaware and rammed by ships.

A Big and Untrustworthy Family

The many varieties of sharks, their feeding habits and ferocity or the lack of it, are indicated by the four species on these pages. They point up the fact that by no means all the sharks are man-eaters—of some 225 to 250 species, only 12 are true and constant menaces—but they also emphasize that few sharks can be trusted. With the exception of the whale shark and the basking shark, both plankton browsers so docile that swimmers have ridden on their backs without disturbing them, all sharks are predators with a catholic diet and ravenous appetites. Their staple food is other fishes, but the larger ones also eat sea turtles, seals and even members of their own kind. All carnivorous sharks have a predilection for animals in distress, and this includes dogs, cats, men and even, in an authenticated case, a crazed elephant that ran into the sea.

THE LEMON SHARK, found in warm Atlantic and Indo-Pacific inshore waters, sometimes attacks man. This specimen, with remoras atop its yellowish body, is preceded by a pilotfish.

91

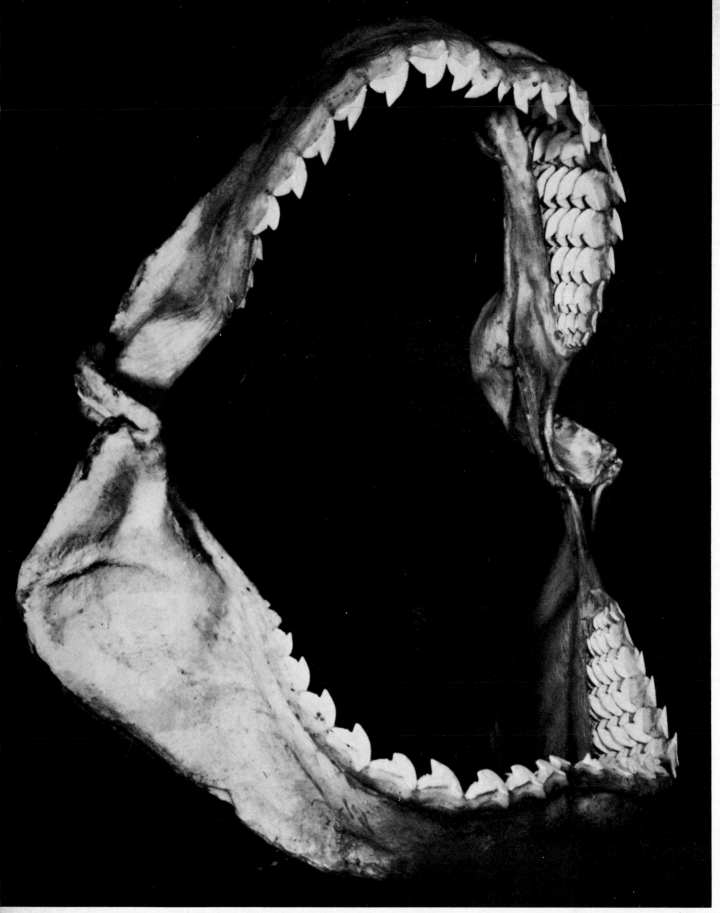

THE TEETH OF A TIGER SHARK, serrated for efficient cutting, rim its cartilaginous jaws. When those in front drop out or are lost, teeth in the second row move into place. The spare teeth are always larger than those in use, and in this way keep up with the shark's growth. During a period of 10 years, a tiger shark may produce, use and shed some 24,000 triangular teeth.

THE VERTEBRAL COLUMN OF A SKATE SHOWS ELABORATE CALCIFICATION, EVEN THOUGH, LIKE ITS COUSIN THE SHARK, IT LACKS TRUE BONES

With Not a Bone in Its Body

The shark's skeleton is composed of cartilage, which disintegrates far more rapidly than bone and is poor material for fossilization. As a result, the record the sharks have left behind them is vague. Most shark fossils consist of teeth and spines, or a few calcified vertebrae and brain cases. Rare is a well-preserved fossil of the entire animal, like that of the shark's relative, *Xiphotrygon* (meaning "sword sting ray"), shown in the photograph below. Some of the best fossils of the earliest sharks were found in the late Devonian shale deposits of Ohio and consisted of little more than impressions of the skin and body shape, and traces of the muscle and kidney tissue.

But sometimes, even on the basis of such a meager clue as a handful of fossilized teeth, paleontologists can deduce the nature of the shark to which they belonged—only, however, when the teeth bear some resemblance to those of a modern shark. This is not always as frustrating as it might seem, since living types include such archaic species as the Port Jackson shark, which goes back 181 million years, the cow shark, dating back 166 million years, and a cat shark with the Latin name *Galeus melastomus* and a history of 136 million years. In fact, as long as 63 million years ago, all the contemporary families of sharks, skates and rays had come into being.

A FOSSILIZED FAN-SHAPED STING RAY FROM WYOMING IS ABOUT 58 MILLION YEARS OLD, BUT IT DIFFERS LITTLE FROM THE RAYS OF TODAY

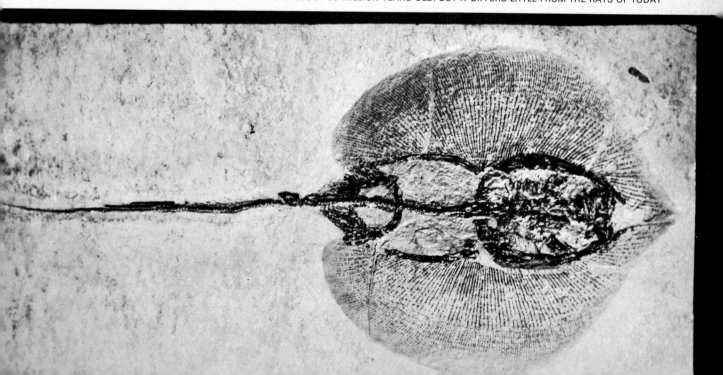

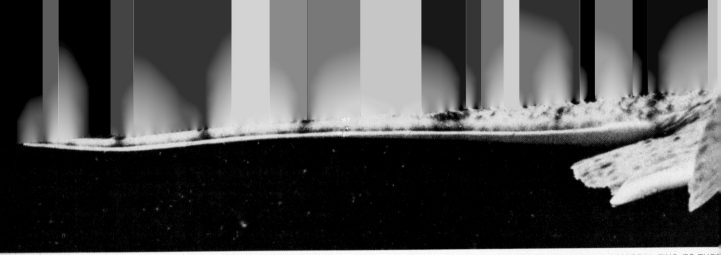

The Supple Skates and Rays

The skates and the rays, though belonging to the same order as the sharks, are higher on the evolutionary tree and differ from them in several ways, principally in swimming. The sharks undulate their bodies, propelling themselves by creating concave surfaces in the water against which to push. The skates and rays, with such exceptions as the sawfish *(right)* and the guitarfishes, use their pectoral fins to swim. These are broadened and lengthened at the expense of the caudal and dorsal fins, and they are attached to the head. This gives their owners their characteristic leaflike or butterfly shape. When a skate swims, a wave begins at the foremost edge of the fins and sweeps backward, as in the photograph above. A surface for pushing is provided, and the fish glides forward in a beautiful rippling movement.

THE TEXAS SKATE, a bottom dweller, shows the extended pectoral fins that help set the skates and rays apart from the sharks. Its flat shape is an adaptation to the environment, as are the spiracles, near the eyes, through which the skate draws water.

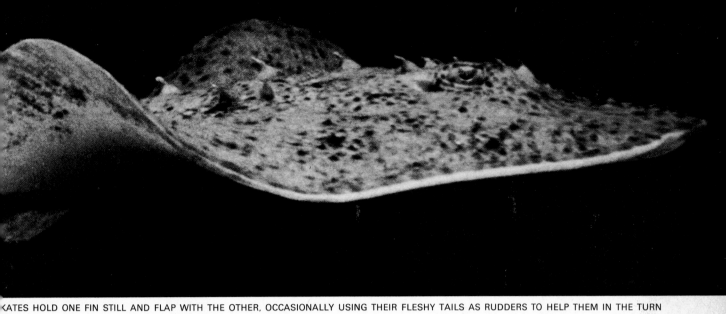

SKATES HOLD ONE FIN STILL AND FLAP WITH THE OTHER, OCCASIONALLY USING THEIR FLESHY TAILS AS RUDDERS TO HELP THEM IN THE TURN

SHARK, WITH MIGHTY STROKES OF ITS TAIL AND THE END OF ITS TRUNK. TYPICALLY ITS SNOUT MAY BE EDGED WITH 15 TO 30 PAIRS OF SAW TEETH

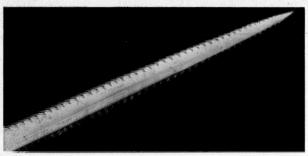

THE POISON SPINE of a southern sting ray is notched with a row of tiny barbs. Primitive men throughout the world use these spines as needles and for spear tips, and the tails as whips.

Beware: Poison

While some rays use electric shocks to ward off their enemies, others, like the species shown on these pages, rely on their poisonous barbed tails for defense. The tails, usually longer than the bodies, are flexible, and the rays wield them like whips, switching them sideways or snapping them up over their heads. The barbs are located along the tail and, in some cases, as in the cow-nosed ray at right, at the base. They release a venom that affects the vascular system of a victim and brings on swelling and violent cramps or, if the swimmer's abdomen has been slashed, may even cause death. The young are born alive, with the barbs flexible and in a sheath. This prevents injury to the mother during birth. The same is true of the toothed saw of the baby sawfish.

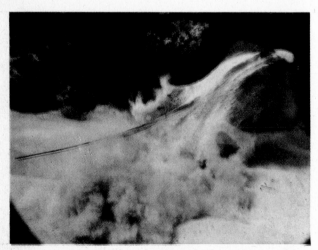

IN A CLOUD OF SAND, a southern sting ray flashes its dangerous tail. Rays, which feed on crustaceans, clams and small fishes, use their pectoral fins to dig for bivalves buried in the sand.

IN FLYING FORMATION, an armada of cow-nosed rays trails long rapierlike tails. Their spines are located so close to their bodies that they are less efficient than those of the sting rays.

5

The Complexities
of Reproduction

To fishes, as to any living thing, the reproduction of their own kind is second in importance only to feeding and sustaining life. In the aquatic world, it is a comparatively simple matter for most species—when the time comes, male and female need merely shed their eggs and sperm into the water where, as they mingle in clouds, fertilization occurs. But in any group of creatures as extraordinarily diverse as the fishes, there are, of course, always exceptions to the general rule, and so in the waters of the world some surprisingly complex and ingenious ways of assuring a continuing population are to be found.

Basically, the reproductive organs of fishes are no different from those of any other animal. In both sexes the gonads, or sperm- and egg-producing organs, are carried in elongated, paired sacs which run lengthwise in the body cavity above and behind the other internal organs (commercially, the egg sacs of the female are known as hard roe, the creamy milt of the male as soft roe). Eggs and sperm may be discharged directly to the exterior through ducts; sometimes, however, the eggs are dropped into the body cavity from where they pass out to the water through genital pores. If fertilization is internal, the eggs are kept inside the body. In most fishes, the size of the reproductive organs is relatively enormous compared to other animals—in the female salmon, for example, the ovaries may make up one fifth to one fourth of the total body weight of the fish.

The predetermination of sex in fishes is a more haphazard and labile affair than in the higher vertebrates, and changes in sex and hermaphroditism are occasionally found. Aquarium owners, for instance, may find their swordtails, bettas and paradise fish changing from female to male. In two well-known food-fish families, the porgy and the bass, hermaphrodites are frequent, and some species are always self-fertilizing.

For obvious reasons, the temperature of the water plays a vital role in the reproductive process. Most species have their own favorable temperature range for spawning, and if this varies excessively they may not spawn at all or, at best, be only partially successful. Nor is the danger past when a spawning has been completed—eggs and young are both sensitive to heat and cold, and abrupt temperature changes can wipe out an entire run.

IT follows, therefore, that most fishes have a particular spawning season when the temperature is most likely to be right for them. For the sea herring, which generally stays in northern waters, the spring and the fall are best, and it spawns twice a year at these times. The farther-ranging menhaden, by contrast, chooses its season depending on where it is—off southern New England, these fish usually spawn in June, with a few individuals holding off until August, but farther south off Chesapeake Bay the spawning peak comes in the fall, and still farther south in early winter. In the tropics, many species of fish spawn throughout the year, while others time their spawning according to the warmest months. Thus the lagoon fishes of Mauritius usually spawn in October or November, when the water turns warm after the southwest monsoons, and again in April, before they begin.

Most fishes not only have definite spawning times but also particular spawning grounds where they assemble when the time comes. The cod spawns in shoal waters, normally in depths of 28 to 30 fathoms, and has certain banks where it does so. Off Cape May, New Jersey, there is a particular spawning concentration of cod each winter which actually supports a small, local codfishery. Around the Lofoten Islands off the coast of Norway, there is a great cod spawning ground, and there are other well-known grounds along the Greenland coast, on

FROM MACE TO MONSTER

The larvae of some fishes, like the ocean sunfishes shown here, are so different from the adults that they were often mistakenly classified as distinct species. Soon after hatching, the minuscule (one-eighth-inch) sunfish develops a suit of armor which resembles the business end of a medieval mace (A, B). In one species, five spines grow into long, horny spikes (C). Another transformation leaves the one-inch fish deeper than it is long, with its spines shortened and with a single new tail fin (D). Retaining this shape, it grows into an adult which may weigh as much as a ton and measure 11 feet in length (E).

A

B

the Grand Banks and around Iceland. And, of course, there are the classic examples of anadromous species such as the salmon, shad and alewife which return to the same spawning beds in the same rivers year after year.

While it is easy enough in the aquatic world to ensure that eggs and sperm come together, the survival of the fertilized egg, and the young fishes after they hatch, is another and far more perilous matter. Youth is a time of special danger for all living things, and for fishes particularly so. But nature has ways of making sure that at least enough young survive to perpetuate the race. Special protection may be provided for the egg and young, or the eggs may be produced in such vast numbers that no matter what may befall them some at least are sure to survive.

Fishes, in most cases, have adopted the second alternative. Eggs are shed into the water in staggering quantities and simply left to the mercy of the environment. A 54-pound ling once caught carried 28,361,000 eggs; a 17-pound turbot had nine million. The cod regularly deposits between four and six million eggs at a single spawning—if they all survived each year it would take only a few years to pack all the world's oceans tight with codfish. As it is, less than one egg in every million needs to produce an adult in order to continue the race. All the rest may and do succumb to the many perils of the sea. They are eaten by birds, fishes and a multitude of other enemies, or may drift into water too deep, warm or cold for their further development, or be washed ashore to dry up.

THE eggs of most food fishes go through their development while afloat. Such pelagic eggs are generally small translucent spheres averaging about one millimeter in diameter, surrounded by a transparent membrane, often with one or more globules of oil in each egg to keep it afloat. Some pelagic eggs have special arrangements for attaching themselves to floating objects or each other. Those of most flyingfishes have long filaments which become entangled with the sargassum weed; needlefish eggs have small projections so that they cling together in clumps. The eggs of the herring and of many fresh-water fishes, on the other hand, sink to the bottom when shed. Herring eggs are coated with a sticky substance which adheres to seaweed, stones or anything with which they may come into contact, but salmon, trout and shad eggs, which are generally shed in swift streams, must be deposited in gravel beds to protect them.

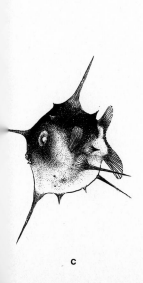

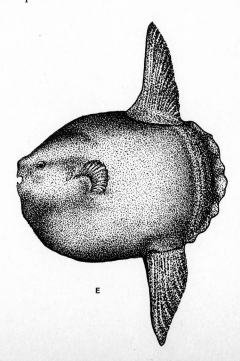

C

D

E

HATCHING A HERRING

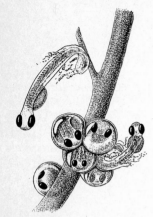

Herring eggs sink to the bottom where they stick to seaweed, stones or sand. There they are relatively safe from the plankton-sifting predators which cruise the upper levels. Once the eggs are anchored, incubation lasts for 11 to 40 days —the colder the water the longer it takes. When they hatch, like some of those attached to the seaweed above, the young consume the yolk sac before beginning a diet of tiny plankton. As adults, the herrings eat larger plankton and shrimps.

Like eggs in general, most fish eggs have a yolk on which the embryo can feed during incubation and even, in some species, for a considerable period after hatching. Once the yolk is used up, the little fish develops a functional mouth and begins to feed itself, taking in microscopic plankton.

In these earliest life stages the fry is usually referred to as a larva, a term used to denote any young animal which has to undergo a greater or lesser transformation to reach its adult form. Sometimes the larvae of fishes may be so utterly different from the adult, both in appearance and habits, that they are unrecognizable as the young of the adults they are destined to become. In many cases these dissimilar larvae were not at first spotted for what they were, but were thought to be quite distinct animals and were given separate names. Such was the case, for example, with an eel larva which until fairly recent history was known as *Leptocephalus* and accepted as a distinct genus all its own.

The larval cod is more typical: though still incomplete, it is recognizable as the fish it will be. It is about a quarter of an inch long when the yolk sac disappears, and at that point may be said to be fully independent, fending for and feeding itself. The fry of the haddock, on the other hand, also a member of the cod family, have worked out a protective arrangement for this critical phase of their lives with a big jellyfish, common to the North Atlantic in the summer: they seek shelter among the stinging tentacles of the cyanea, as these great pale bells are known, and forage for food in safety without getting stung themselves.

THE cod fry may drift and grow for as long as two and a half months before they move, around midsummer, purposefully down to the bottom in shallow inshore water. At this point they are recognizable young fish about three quarters of an inch long, and they begin to feed on small crustaceans. As they grow they move out to deeper water, and at the end of the first year in the North Atlantic they will have reached a length of about six inches. At three years of age they are about a foot long; at this stage, when they are known as codlings, they are already taken in trawls. The young cod finally mature in their fourth or fifth year, when they have reached a length of two or three feet—then, but only then, are they themselves ready to spawn for the first time.

This is fairly typical of the early life of any fish which, like most of our food fishes, sheds pelagic eggs. Once afloat in the water, the eggs naturally drift away on the currents, but the young of many species come together again on nursery grounds. These nurseries are nearly always in shallow water where the depth is less than 20 fathoms. They are therefore nearly always inshore. It is because of this that nations like Iceland, whose livelihood depends almost entirely on fisheries, wish to extend their territorial limits and take action to preserve these young fishes until they move out into deeper water where they can spawn at least once before being swept up in a trawl.

The prodigal system of shedding vast quantities of eggs and simply casting them adrift is well suited to the marine fishes of the offshore or open seas, but there are a number of other species living in more protected waters which have developed more economical ways of producing young. As a rule, such fishes shed only a small number of eggs. Some may seek out hiding places to deposit them, others may keep the eggs inside the body until they are hatched, and some, after the hatching, will even actively guard the young fry until they can fend for themselves.

Most of these unfishlike breeding habits have been adopted by species which live among rocks, in tidal basins, bays and inlets, or in fresh-water streams and lakes. The hazards here are different ones from the open sea—the battering surf of the shoreline, or tides and currents which may wash the eggs into unsuitable areas. There are, however, various ways to protect the eggs, and the ocean pout, a fish often taken in trawls in the western North Atlantic, has ingeniously combined at least two of them.

The ocean pout lays a few hundred very large eggs, six to seven millimeters in diameter, that are bound together in a gelatinous mass. These clumps of eggs have been found in cans, old rubber boots and similar debris dredged up from the ocean floor, strongly suggesting that the female deliberately seeks out a safe hole for her eggs. It is possible that if no safe place is available the female may herself guard the eggs—in any case, one female in an aquarium was observed curled protectively around her egg cluster, which unfortunately in this case proved to be infertile. And a closely related species occurring in European waters, *Zoarces viviparus*, gives birth to its young alive. The eggs are fertilized internally and retained in the oviduct until hatched.

Internal fertilization and retention of the eggs in the oviduct occur in several quite unrelated groups of fishes. This is, of course, characteristic of sharks and rays, but the far smaller and perennially popular guppies and mollies also give birth to their young alive. And so does one very important commercial species in the North Atlantic, the redfish. The redfish is a deep-water species that gives birth to several thousand young, which rise to the surface and spend their first months there sharing the vicissitudes of the environment with the cod fry.

In most of the live bearers, the eggs develop without depending on the mother for other than water and minerals. Such eggs are well supplied with yolk and under these circumstances the development is termed ovoviviparous. At the other extreme, the eggs have no yolk and some or even most of the food required for the embryo's growth is supplied by the mother. Such species are termed viviparous. The developing embryos may be supplied with nutrients in many ways, including a placenta and an umbilicus quite comparable in function and form to that of mammals. Such is the case with the European dogfish, which carries its young for about 10 months. In other species food is supplied to the embryo through its fins, or through special tissue extensions, or through ducts leading from the mother's uterus into the mouth and gills of the embryo.

T HE American gaff-topsail catfish (so called from its curious back fin shaped like a gaff-topsail of a sailing ship) and the tropical spiny sea catfish lay some 50 eggs, each about a quarter of an inch in diameter. The male fish then takes them in his mouth where they develop, living on their own yolk, while their father goes without any food at all until they hatch.

In the so-called "obstetrical catfish" of South America, by contrast, it is the female that assumes the role of protector, carrying the eggs about on her belly. The eggs are equipped with a special stalk to attach them to the mother fish.

The mouth-breeding habit is not restricted to catfishes. Certain species of the popular aquarium family of Cichlidae, especially the Egyptian mouthbreeder and the large mouthbreeder, have variously adopted this technique as well. The eggs are usually deposited initially in a clean depression, shortly after which one parent picks them up and holds them in its mouth at least through the incubation period. In the case of the Egyptian mouthbreeder, it is the female which carries the eggs; in the tilapia the male performs this duty. The parents at various times may seem to be chewing during the incubation period, but these are cleaning actions; they do not feed. The young may return to their

CHANGES OF FORM

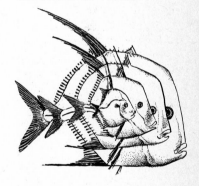

Although some fishes may change shape completely from larva to adult, the lookdown shown here is an example of fishes which undergo only slight modifications. The most conspicuous changes occur in the shape and relative size of the dorsal, anal and pelvic fins. The young lookdown's pelvic and first dorsal fins are almost as long as the fish itself, but they shrink as the fish grows, while the leading edges of the anal and second dorsal fins sprout long streamers which trail from the adult.

SOME STRANGE WAYS OF PROTECTING EGGS

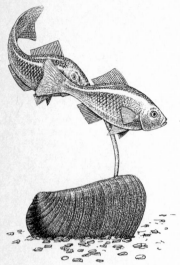

THE BITTERLING

The female bitterling, whose oviduct is drawn out into a long tube, deposits eggs in a fresh-water mussel (above). The male sheds its sperm nearby and, as the shellfish feeds, drawing in water, the eggs are fertilized. The mussel reciprocates by throwing out its own embryos into the water where they attach themselves parasitically to adult fishes, usually on the gills.

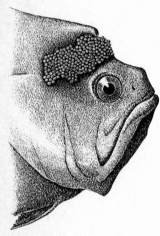

THE KURTUS

The male Australian Kurtus has a unique adaptation: it incubates eggs on its forehead. As the young male grows to maturity, its dorsal-fin spines move forward to form a hook. It is believed this hook detaches the eggs from aquatic plants after they are fertilized. Two clusters of eggs, fixed with sticky filaments at both ends of a strand, are firmly secured by this hook.

mouth haven until they get too big, but beyond a certain point they do so at their peril, for their parent may eat them too.

An extremely complex behavioral pattern associated with breeding has been observed in pipefishes and seahorses. Pipefishes are common in warm temperate and tropical waters, especially on beds of eelgrass. They may reach a length of 18 inches, but in the tropics they are usually a good deal smaller. They swim almost vertically, often bent into an S shape, advancing sedately by undulations of their dorsal fins, with an arrogant expression on their long tubular snouts. When feeding, they twine their tails around fronds of weed and probe inquisitively about for small crustaceans.

The male Florida pipefish grows flaps along his underside which, at the breeding season, fuse together and form a pouch (other kinds of pipefish have a groove on their undersides lined by soft skin). When mating takes place the male and female approach and tentatively pass one another a few times, then link S's, crossing in three places. The male caresses the female with his snout, usually on her belly, and she, with her protruding oviduct, neatly deposits her eggs in his pouch, or abdominal groove, where they are fertilized. The male then does a sort of gyrating, spiraling dance in order to pack the eggs down in rows, after which they repeat the performance until the pouch is full. The female then swims away, her role fulfilled, leaving the male entirely responsible for the process of gestation. In about two weeks the father's pouch is full of perfectly formed young pipefish. The walls of the pouch then open up and the small, threadlike young emerge and take to the water with the same stately deportment as their parents. They may return to the safety of their father's pouch, or groove, when danger threatens.

The seahorse, which is a close relative of the pipefish, carries its head at right angles to its hunched body, giving it a diminished, horsy look. The male also carries the young in a brood pouch under the tail where they are fed from the father's blood supply. However, in this case the pouch does not rupture. Instead, when the young are ready, the father coils his tail around a frond of weed and undergoes, apparently, all the pangs of giving birth. He bends sharply backward and forward, contracting the muscles of the wall of the pouch and, at each spasm, a tiny young seahorse is shot out, perfectly formed, into the water.

Some fishes quite deliberately lay their eggs out of the water. The characin *Copeina arnoldi*, at home in the Amazon River and its tributaries, has gone to unusual extremes to assure the survival of its eggs. After a preliminary courtship, the male escorts the female to a spot where a leaf or branch overhangs the surface of the water by an inch or two. The pair lock fins and leap out of the water, clinging to the leaf for an instant to deposit a small mass of eggs. This act is performed repeatedly until a sizable number of eggs is attached to the leaf. To prevent the eggs from drying out, the male fish periodically splashes them with his tail during their three-day hatching period.

The bitterling of central Europe has developed a spawning behavioral pattern fully as unique in a different way. The eggs are deposited in the gill chamber of fresh-water mussels. This is accomplished in a most unusual manner. The female develops a very long ovipositor, which is inserted into the gill chamber of the mussel to leave the eggs. It is an act of highly developed instinctive behavior that the ovipositor can be so inserted without the mussel clamping down on it. Once safely deposited in this unusual nest, the eggs are fertilized by the male sperm which, released into the water around the mussel, is pumped into it along with the mussel's food. The mussel itself does not seem to mind a bit being the host to these alien eggs.

The grunion, surf smelt, capelin and even occasionally the sand launce have abandoned the water as a place of safekeeping for their eggs and go all out to deposit them on the shore. Of all these, the grunion is the best known for its dramatic spawning habits. It spawns from March to August on certain California beaches during the periods of higher tides associated with new and full moons, laying its eggs in the sand at the upper reaches of the tide. The female, at precisely the correct moment between waves, buries herself tailfirst in the sand and deposits the eggs. The nearest male sheds his sperm about her and the eggs are fertilized. Two weeks later, during the next series of high tides, the eggs are washed out of the sand and hatch explosively.

Grunions are known to spawn more than once, every two weeks on each cycle of high water. The timing of this activity is amazing to observe. They carefully wait until the tide has just passed its peak, beginning the deposition of eggs on the second night following the highest point of the tidal cycle, thus assuring that the next cycle of high tides will expose the eggs and allow them to hatch.

Tнᴇ nest-building and tending habits of fresh-water fishes, especially pan fishes, are well known to any angler. The nesting behavior of the ubiquitous and pretty little pumpkinseed is fairly typical of the group. When spawning time approaches late in the spring, the male noticeably brightens and begins to scoop out a shallow depression in the water close inshore. When the nest is ready, he finds a female ready to spawn and escorts her. Once she has laid her eggs, he drives her away and looks for another. Thus any one male's nest may contain the eggs of several females, and any one female may spawn several times during the summer. While the eggs are developing, the male defends the nest against all comers. His strong protective instinct is often the pumpkinseed's downfall—if a fishhook drops on his nest, he will pick it up to remove it, so that a lot of pumpkinseed are caught during the hatching period. The male may watch over the newly hatched young for a short time, but his interest soon lags and the young fish are on their own.

The common bullhead, or horned pout, is an especially protective parent. The female lays a few thousand fairly large eggs in an especially constructed hole or an old muskrat tunnel. The male guards, cleans and ventilates the mass of eggs throughout the incubation period which usually lasts about a week. The young hatch out as small, jet-black replicas of their parents, form into large schools and proceed to explore their new home, closely followed and guarded by the male. The male bullhead may continue to chaperon the school until the babies are as much as two inches long.

Not all fishes have a simple depression on the bottom for a nest. There are nests made of bubbles and others so well constructed of bits and pieces of vegetation as to put some birds to shame.

The Asiatic family Anabantidae, although not large, includes a number of species popular with the aquarist, especially the gouramis and the Siamese fighting fish. The male builds the nest by producing small bubbles in his mouth. A small amount of mucus goes into the manufacture of these bubbles, making them less fragile than ordinary soap-and-water bubbles. In the wild, the nests are usually built up under some object, such as a leaf, floating on the surface.

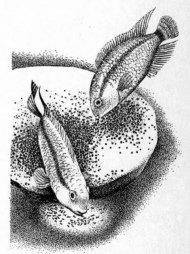

When enough bubbles have accumulated, courtship follows. The male places the eggs in this nest, guarding and tending it. He is kept very busy since it is constantly in need of repair. In addition to being beautifully colored, the males have a strong protective instinct for their nesting territory and will protect it against all comers—which is why this betta has won such fame for its pugilistic prowess.

But perhaps no nesting routine among fishes is more formal or elaborate than that of the common stickleback native to our own ponds and streams. In northern Europe and America there are several stickleback species, each distinguished by the number of isolated spines along the back. They inhabit both brackish and fresh water, and one lives in salt water on the seashore just below the high-tide mark.

THE breeding routine of the various sticklebacks begins when the male builds a very fine nest in a quiet-flowing channel among weeds. The nest is tubular and made of bits of stems, roots and other fragments of aquatic plants. He binds these together with a sticky secretion of his own kidneys and shapes the nest by rubbing himself against the material. The secretion hardens to a cement in the water. He also throws some sand onto the base of the nest to make a sort of foundation. When completed, his home is quite a neat-looking tunnel with a front and back entrance and a clear stream of water flowing through it. The nest takes the male several days to construct and then the important business of finding a mate begins.

As the courtship approaches, the three-spined stickleback, normally blue or green with silver belly, flushes red below. The 10-spined and the 15-spined, normally green, turn dark brown and blue respectively. Thus attractively dressed, the male approaches the female of his choice, driving off rival males with great ferocity. He coaxes her, with a mixture of force and persuasion, to the nest. She deposits two or three eggs and then impolitely pushes her way out, or is chased out by the male. This is repeated with a string of brides until the nest is full of eggs. Then the male stands guard over it for nearly a month, chasing away all intruders, including his former mates. He repairs the fabric, and aerates the eggs with his pectoral fins. When the young are hatched he dismantles the nest, except for the foundation which remains as a cradle for the fry, and guards the young until they can fend for themselves.

When it comes to adapting breeding practice to habitat, no stranger example can be found than that of the deep-water anglerfishes. They spend all their lives at depths where almost total darkness prevails (like our common angler, or frogfish, of shallower coastal areas, they angle for their prey with a rod and bait, but the bait is luminous and can be switched on and off at will). In these dark depths the chances of boy meeting girl are remote, so it seems not illogical that the females should carry their males about with them. Almost as soon as they are hatched the young males fix themselves by their mouths to any part of the female's body. The male's mouth is pincerlike and not gaping like that of the female, and once he has fastened himself, the tissues of his mouth fuse completely with those of the female. There may even be more than one male thus attached and carried around by a female. The male never grows but remains throughout life a dwarf, fed by his mate's blood stream and with only his reproductive organs fully developed and functioning to assure the continuation of the species in the stygian waters far beneath the surface of the sea.

A PAIR OF YELLOW-HEADED JAWFISH FROM THE FLORIDA REEFS NOD AND SWAY TO EACH OTHER IN WHAT APPEARS TO BE A COURTSHIP DANCE

The Way to Parenthood

Reproduction among land animals centers around a single well-integrated act. But long before any animal walked on land, this act, as the fishes on the following pages demonstrate, evolved out of many separate steps, each of which represented a great advance in behavior or physiology. Basic as it seems, the first advance was for male to meet female—as the two jawfish are doing above.

THE NORMAL LIVERY of the male cuckoo wrasse, a foot-long marine fish that ranges from Norway to Italy, shows delicately shaded colors that the wrasse wears for 11 months of the year.

THE MATING COLORS of the same fish in springtime are totally different (below), standing out in bold patterns accentuated by a dramatic blanching around the neck and shoulders.

FINNY FINERY is flaunted by a six-inch male dragonet as it puffs up its back and gill covers to court a drab female. These unusually ceremonious little fish spawn off the coast of Europe.

Courtship and Its Culmination

A million naked eggs set adrift in a dangerous ocean, a million sperm frantically wriggling through the waters to hunt them down—this prodigally wasteful saturation technique used by so many fishes in their reproduction is vastly improved by one simple act: courtship. By courtship, as the two little European coastal fishes on these pages illustrate, mates come together to perform their spawning rite in a purposeful and synchronized manner which cuts down colossally on the number of eggs that must be produced and improves the chances for survival.

The male cuckoo wrasse (*opposite*) goes about its courting with tyrannical directness. Changing color and looking fierce, he threshes out a hollow in the sand for a nest and darts about biting and bumping the females in the area until one of them is frightened or fascinated into coming with him and filling his nest with eggs.

The dragonet (*right and above*) goes a-wooing less ferociously. He captivates his partner by showing off his bright colors and flamboyant fins, then fertilizes her eggs as she lays them by taking a swim with her toward the surface of the sea. After this tender ritual is over, the eggs float up to incubate in the oceanic plankton while both parents abandon them to hatch and survive as best they are able.

A SLOW BALLET consummates the mating as male and female dragonet swim upward, their fins gently touching, while the male releases sperm around the new-laid eggs.

Homes for the Unhatched

Instead of abandoning their eggs, some of the more highly developed fishes take active steps to protect the jellies they have laid through the incubation and hatching period. The famous upriver runs of salmon are carried out so that their eggs can be laid in rushing, gravel-bedded headwaters where predators are few and the fry can go through their early, defenseless stages in comparative safety before following their parents back to the sea. The Brazilian discus fish (*below*) actively guards its eggs until they hatch and even watches over the school of fry for a while afterward. The male banded pipefish (*opposite, below*) goes a step further: it holds and hatches the eggs in a tissue-lined groove of its belly. Other pipefishes carry the eggs in a pouch under the tail.

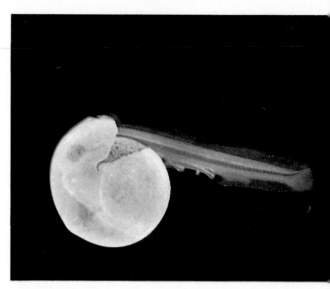

A SALMON EGG from a Nova Scotia fish nursery begins to hatch as the embryo's tiny tail breaks through the egg membrane and is pulled out straight by the current of the cold stream water.

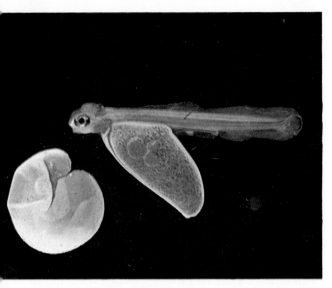

THE SALMON EMBRYO emerges fully, looking more like some dragonfly larva than a fish. The yellow "wing" on its underside is actually the egg's yolk, its only food source for weeks to come.

THE FINAL STAGE of larval life is reached when the egg yolk is nearly exhausted. Then the tiny but almost perfect salmon opens its mouth and takes in microscopic sustenance for itself.

BANDED PIPEFISH EGGS, LAID BY THE FEMALE AT RIGHT, ARE FERTILIZED, CARRIED, NURSED AND HATCHED ON THE MALE'S BELLY AT LEFT

TRANSPARENT EGGS, inconspicuous against colored backgrounds, are laid by a discus fish on an orange board. The parents move the hatching eggs by mouth to hiding places.

The Burden of Fatherhood

Since fish eggs are laid first and fertilized second, the task of incubating the eggs and rearing the fry is most likely to fall—if at all—upon the fertilizing parent, the one who sees the eggs last, the father. One of the most straightforward ways for a male fish to shoulder this responsibility is with its mouth, as demonstrated below by the little tilapia that lives in African rivers and Indonesian ponds. After fertilizing a clutch of eggs, a male tilapia goes on a fortnight's fast and dedicates its mouth first as a hatchery and then as a haven for the fry to run to while they are learning to take care of themselves. Later, of course, if one of the fry becomes tied to the paternal apron strings and swims back too often, it eventually is swallowed by its hungry father.

SAFEGUARDING THE HATCH, a male tilapia scoops eggs into its mouth from a nest built previously by its mate and filled and fertilized in a sequence of dive-bombing passes by both parents.

INCUBATING THE EGGS, the male tilapia gapes gingerly as it protects its ripening orange mouthful. It takes about five days for the eggs to hatch and another six or eight for the young fish to complete enough of their embryonic development so that they can cope with life. All this time the hungry male restrains its jaw-closing impulses and lives off its dwindling stores of body fat.

SPITTING OUT FRY in helter-skelter, head-over-tail profusion, the male tilapia finally relinquishes its young to the tests of survival. Speedy breeders and careful parents, tilapias can multiply with enormous rapidity. Introduced into the heavily fished ponds of some underdeveloped nations, they are expected to become a popular source of inexpensive protein food.

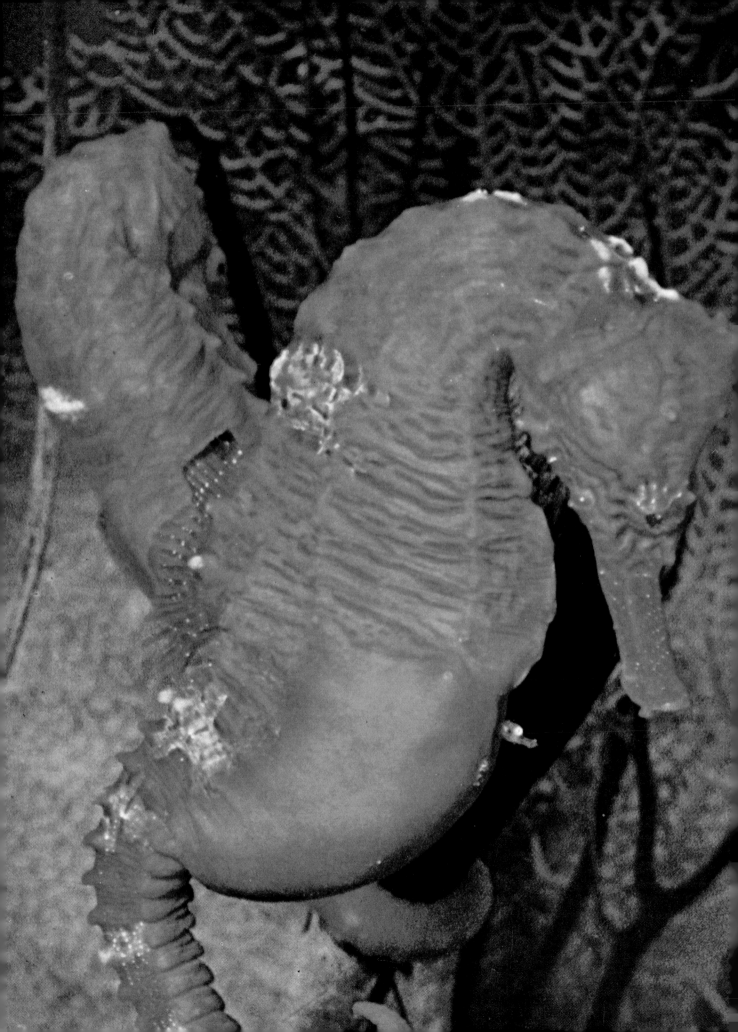

Maternal Males and Females

Since a father's mouth is at best an awkward place to hatch eggs, a few highly evolved fishes have developed special organs to serve as primitive wombs. The paternal brood pouch of the seahorse (*opposite*) enables its young to pass their embryonic days inside their father. In the fresh-water molly, evolution has hit on the maternal scheme used by higher animals. The male molly fertilizes the eggs while they are still within the female and there, without ever being laid, the eggs hatch and the fry develop.

A PREGNANT MOLLY delivers diminutive young fully formed. Since they were fertilized within her, they never had to run the usual fish-egg gantlet of exposure to the outside world.

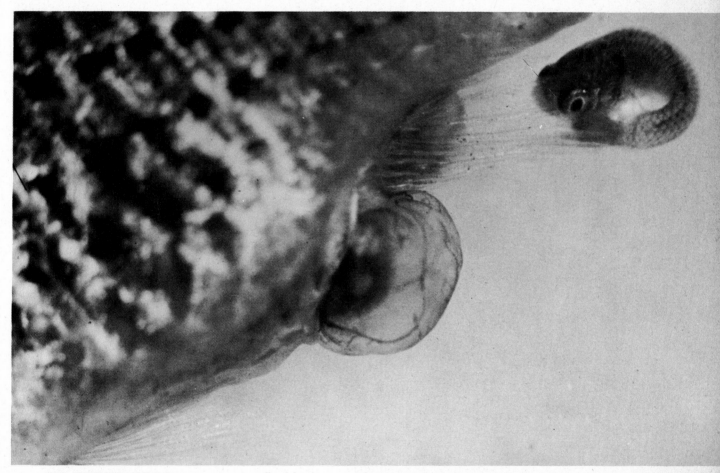

INTO ITS WATER WORLD goes a young molly (*above*). At birth, mollies are far better equipped to survive than species from externally laid eggs, but one danger they face is their father who, released from his instinctual responsibilities, sometimes swallows the babies (*right*).

THE BIRTH OF A SEAHORSE (*opposite*) reveals the head of a young one poking from the brood pouch of its father. This pouch, which probably evolved from ridges in the skin like the pipefish's on page 111, is filled with eggs by the female and stays swollen for 8 to 10 days of gestation.

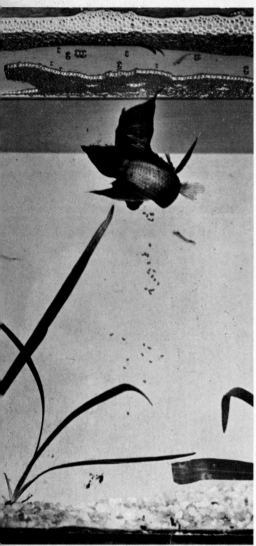

THE TEMPESTUOUS COURTSHIP of two bettas reaches a climax when the male squeezes its partner into laying eggs. It fertilizes the sinking eggs *(left)*, then fetches them from the bottom in its mouth *(center)* and sticks them into a floating nest of foamy mucous bubbles *(right)* which it built beforehand. Now it guards the nest against all comers, including the mother.

Defenders of the Nest

Fishes which have not evolved internal ways of protecting their helpless eggs and fry often achieve the same ends with sharp teeth, bad tempers and zealous parental instincts. The male of the Siamese fighting fish, *Betta splendens* above, guards its nest with such ferocity that in its native Thailand it is counted on—and gambled on—to fight like a game-cock against other males of its species. Because of its sporting nature, it has been bred into the long-finned, rainbow-hued pet of modern fish fanciers, but originally it was a drab thing with ordinary fins. Mating begins for it in a rough-and-tumble chase after the female, which often leaps from the

water in flight. Once reduced to submissiveness, it is periodically nipped and butted until ready to lay eggs. Then the male wraps itself around its mate and appears literally to squeeze the eggs from its body. It then dismisses the female and takes up a ferocious vigil near the nest, continuing this until the hatched fry are six days old.

The Amazonian discus fish opposite is also a game defender of its young, but in this case both male and female participate. While the eggs are incubating, both parents mouth them and fan them with fins and, after hatching, continue to watch over them carefully until they are able to swim.

A MALE DISCUS FISH does convoy duty for its school of tiny fry as they play and ply their way through the dangerous water. When the young fish are not swimming they are feeding on nutritious secretions from special cells in the parental skin. If either parent gets tired of them, it passes the entire confettilike cluster on to its mate by a single flick of the body.

A BLACK BULLHEAD, carrying the reproductive process almost to the point of educating its young, cruises with its school of scholars while they learn the ropes of life. The male (and on rare occasions, the female) serves in this guard and guide duty—which may be why bullheads are among the most plentiful catfish species in North America. This black variety is usually found in the silted backwaters and overflow ponds along the creeks and rivers of the Midwest.

6

Life and Death
in a
Silent Realm

IN the vast, dim submarine world inhabited by the fishes, competition for the basic necessities of life is every bit as fierce as it is among the animals which live on land. Any shallow pond or lakeside, any tidal pool will show its horde of little creatures feeding on the tiny bottom plants and plankton. These are the food-rich areas, with plenty of oxygen from plant photosynthesis, plenty of light, and plenty of living space with sand, mud, weeds and rocks all contributing their share of food and hiding places.

In these shallow areas, the water is a window which reveals to human observers the underwater community of the fishes, invertebrates and plants, crowded closely, often piled on top of one another in the silent, ceaseless warfare of survival—enemies and allies, predators and prey. What is the structure of this community? How do its members get along?

Like other animals, fishes enter into associations with each other and with other underwater creatures. These may be casual relationships or they may be of a very intimate kind. Looking around in the sea, one can trace a series of associations becoming ever closer and more intimate right up to those in which one partner lives entirely at the expense of the other and cannot live any other way.

Some fishes strike up an association with inanimate things. In the warmer waters of the North Atlantic, there lives a fine large fish which has entered into a "relationship" with the flotsam of the sea. It is usually to be found lurking under any large floating object, such as a log, a balk of timber, a kerosene drum. This curious habit has earned it the name wreckfish and, since it is extremely good to eat, fishermen keep an eye out for floating wreckage and flotsam generally and examine it to see if, by luck, there is a wreckfish underneath. The fish, of course, feels no passionate attachment to its piece of flotsam but goes there to eat the barnacles, mussels and any other life which it finds growing on it.

The most obvious relationship between two living animals is that of predator and prey. This begins with the smallest fishes, which are also the most abundant. Predators themselves, which often feed on the zooplankton and other small animals, also serve as prey for the larger and less abundant fishes equipped to eat them. Herrings, pilchards, anchovies in the ocean, shiners in the lakes are all preyed upon by larger fishes such as mackerel, bluefish and bass; and these in turn are prey for the still-larger carnivores like sharks and pikes. This is a relationship which on all levels is direct and final, entered into suddenly and finished quickly, the basis of life—and death—in the waters.

THERE are, of course, many other less drastic relationships both between fishes themselves and between fishes and other organisms in the water. There is the very loose and casual kind of association in which one partner merely takes shelter with the other or benefits in some way, without giving any apparent benefit or, for that matter, inflicting any apparent injury, in return. This is usually termed commensalism, which means literally "being at table together."

In one example of commensalism, small gobies of the east coast of the United States take shelter in empty oyster shells. Once such a goby, seven eighths of an inch long, was found embedded in the gill chamber of a living oyster. This was obviously an accidental association, but strangely enough, the oyster was suffering no ill effects from it. Other gobies shelter in the gill chambers of fishes, and still another goby has gone to an extreme of adaptation—it is blind and lives in the burrow of a shrimplike crustacean upon which it depends entirely for food and a home. A cardinal fish has worked out an accommodation with a big sea snail, living in its mantle cavity. Various young fishes take shelter in the shells of oysters, clams and scallops.

A more literal interpretation of "being at table together" has been adopted by the pilotfish which almost always accompany tropical sharks. The pilotfish is about a foot long, blue in color with darker stripes along its sides. It swims alongside its companion shark just below and behind the head, matching the movements of the big predator with extraordinary precision. Pilotfish were known to the ancient Greeks and Romans, and for a long time were thought to be guiding the sharks to their food. Actually, the opposite is true: what they really appear to do is feed on scraps from the sharks' meals. Nor do they, as was previously thought, attach themselves to a particular shark: on the contrary, if one shark among a group of several takes a bite at something, the pilotfish will swim away from the sharks that are not feeding and join the one that is. As for the shark, it gets no visible benefit from its relationship with the pilotfish, but merely tolerates its presence.

The relationship of the shark sucker, or remora, to its shark companion is not very different from that of the pilotfish except that the remora attaches itself to the shark's body and is carried about by it. There are some 10 different kinds of remoras in tropical waters, ranging in size from a few inches to about three feet. They all have a flat, oval disk on the top of the head evolved from the forward section of the dorsal fin, with a series of 13 to 25 transverse plates, V-shaped and arranged like the slats of a Venetian blind. The remora can stick to any flat surface by applying the disk and then erecting the transverse vanes so as to create a vacuum. It is an extremely efficient adhesive apparatus, so much so that in some tropical islands the natives use remoras to catch turtles, flinging the remora out with a line attached to it and then, when it has fastened onto the turtle, hauling both in. The only way to dislodge a remora is by sliding it forward, since sliding it sideways or backward only tends to raise the slats and increase the vacuum still further.

When the shark is feeding, the remora looses its hold and scavenges around on its own, returning to one shark or another when the meal is over. When a shark is caught and hauled out of the water, its remoras usually drop off and find another shark or, possibly, attach themselves to a ship's hull. Occasionally remoras attach themselves to fishes other than sharks. Certain other species of remoras are found on sporting fishes and in the mouth or gill cavity of the giant sunfish and marlins.

Some young fishes, as previously noted, associate with jellyfish, among them the European whiting, young haddock and crevallés which often shelter under the bells of jellyfish among the coral reefs. A relative of the crevallé live in close association with the Portuguese man-of-war. The sting of this large jellyfish, which drifts about on the surface with its tentacles spread out beneath the surface as a fine, almost invisible network for as much as a hundred feet, can render a man unconscious, but this little fish can go in and out apparently quite unharmed. Nevertheless, this association is not without its dangers: should the fish accidentally brush too roughly against the tentacles, it may be stung and devoured. Presumably the host in this case does not so much tolerate its inmates as live unaware of their existence.

EVEN more extraordinary and more intimate is the relationship between the brilliantly banded anemonefish, a type of damselfish of the tropical coastal reefs, and the giant stinging sea anemones with which they live. The anemone is a pale, deceptively flaccid creature up to three feet in diameter with a tangle of tentacles covered with batteries of stinging cells. It does not form a round rosette like the anemone we see in a rock pool but rather has a wavy shape and fills the crevices and corners of the reef with a spreading, irregular, tentacled mass. Nearly every anemone has three, four or even more anemonefish carrying on their lives among its poisonous arms, darting out on occasional feeding forays but returning always to the protective custody of their landlord. Each fish knows its own anemone and always returns to the same one. Sometimes a male and a female will even keep house together, depositing a pile of eggs next to the anemone. The eggs are zealously cared for by the father while the mother guards against intruders. Upon hatching, the larvae swarm to the surface to feed on plankton for a couple of weeks. Then they return to the bottom, searching for their own anemone hosts. Once it has found an anemone the young fish will go through an acclimatization process by which it gradually acquires immunity from the otherwise lethal tentacles.

It used to be thought that the anemone got nothing out of this relationship, but later evidence suggests that the anemonefish not only bring back offerings of food for the anemone, but also act as decoys for other types of fishes which they lure to their doom in the tentacles. If this is so, it would be a case of mutualism, with the fish getting protection and the anemone occasional meals. But it is also possible that the association goes even further—that it involves a form of servicing arrangement whereby the anemone cleans the fish of minute crustaceans or fungi on its skin. In any case, the anemonefish can be seen turning on their sides as they swim through the tentacles, rubbing against them in what seems almost an affectionate manner, like aquatic cats asking to be scratched.

That there are such servicing arrangements among fishes has been established beyond question. The late Conrad Limbaugh, a conscientious submarine biologist and photographer, was among the first to observe this and to conclude that certain fishes have a well-defined cleaner-client relationship with others. Fishes are often infested with parasites on their skin, mouth and gills. They quite often deliberately seek out those kinds of fishes which perform a cleaning service by feeding on the parasites. Fishes are also susceptible to infections by fungi and bacteria, especially if there is any puncture of the skin. Such infections often appear as furry, white growths near wounds. The cleaners remove these growths together with any dead tissue from the wounds.

Cleaning relationships among land animals are much better known. The little white egret of the tropics sits on top of the water buffalo and removes ticks with its sharp beak, and the story of the Egyptian plover cleaning the teeth of the crocodile on the banks of the Nile has been repeated since the days of Herodotus. William Beebe saw crabs and finches picking ticks from the hides of marine iguanas in the Galápagos. He also observed fishes of the wrasse family cleaning parrotfish off Haiti, and many others have confirmed that the cleaning activities of certain birds and land animals are duplicated under the sea.

Dozens of fish species regularly clean or groom others in both tropical and temperate waters. Besides fishes, several shrimps, a bird, a crab and a worm also make cleaning their profession. However, many cleaners work only part time while others do so only when they are young. Wrasses are among the most diligent of cleaners, but the pilotfish does duty as a cleaner of manta rays too, and a tropical angelfish is so well known for its grooming activities that it is called "the barber" along the Mexican coast. The butterflyfish and the neon

WHO EATS WHOM IN THE SEA

A typical food chain, like the one below, consists of five links, beginning with billions of microscopic plant plankton and ending with relatively small numbers of giant carnivores, like the sharks. The first link is plant plankton, which converts sun energy to organic compounds by photosynthesis and indirectly provides food for the entire community of the sea. These one-celled green plants are eaten by minute animal plankton (mostly crustaceans) which, in turn, are consumed by herring and other small fishes. Larger predaceous fishes, like cod, eat the herring and are finally themselves preyed upon by still larger fishes, represented by the mackerel shark. Here the chain ends, for sharks have no natural enemies other than man.

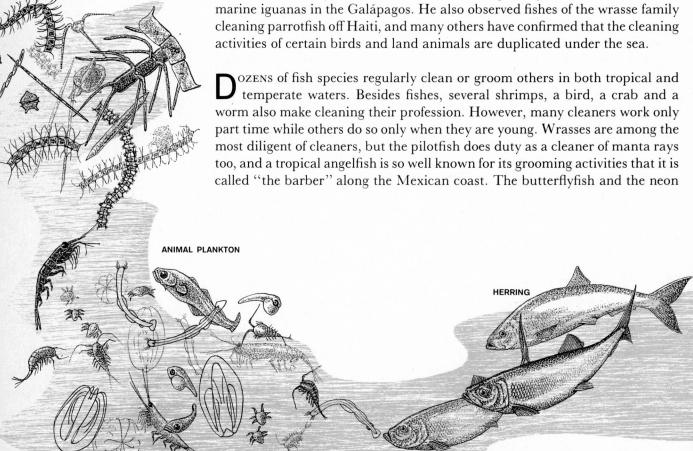

PLANT PLANKTON

ANIMAL PLANKTON

HERRING

goby are also well-known cleaners. Some wrasses and gobies go into a customer's mouth, work over the teeth and even the gullet until their client signifies, by snapping its jaws a few times, that it wants to end the cleaning.

In temperate waters the cleaners are less brightly colored and the relationship, on the whole, is not so highly organized as in the tropics. The cleaners take a greater risk in carrying out their function and quite often find, when the job is done, that the customer is hungry. But sometimes the reverse is true, and the would-be customer finds itself duped by a predator in cleaner's clothing. In the tropical Indian and Pacific oceans, for example, the saber-toothed blenny has assumed the livery of a well-known wrasse cleaner, and goes through all the motions of attracting a client—only to rip into the unfortunate victim with all the ferocity of a pint-sized barracuda.

THE bright colors and strong patterns of the tropical cleaning fishes beyond doubt serve to advertise their profession, but they have other ways of signaling their customers as well. When they see a prospect approaching, they may swim out to meet it and put on a dance. This is a gesture of self-identification rather than aggressive salesmanship, for a cleaner usually finds more clients than it can take care of. One kind of wrasse performs a sort of dance by spreading its tail and waving it up and down. At this point, the client often swims slowly or remains virtually motionless, usually in a peculiar pose, tilting to one side or another, standing on its head or tail. The cleaner then goes to work, methodically making its way up and down the client's body, nibbling minute crustaceans or pecking away at infections. If it wants to get in underneath a fin, the cleaner will gently nudge until it is lifted. It will similarly work its way under the gill covers and probe between lips and teeth to persuade its client to open its mouth so that it can get inside.

The job a cleaner does is a very thorough one, and sometimes a client fish will seem to help it along by changing color to show up sore spots or infestations. An Indian Ocean fish turns from near black to light blue, another simply turns pale. A species of discus fish which seems to be especially afflicted by fungus infections turns almost black so that the white fungi show up clearly.

Usually the tropical cleaner fishes have a definite place of business which be-

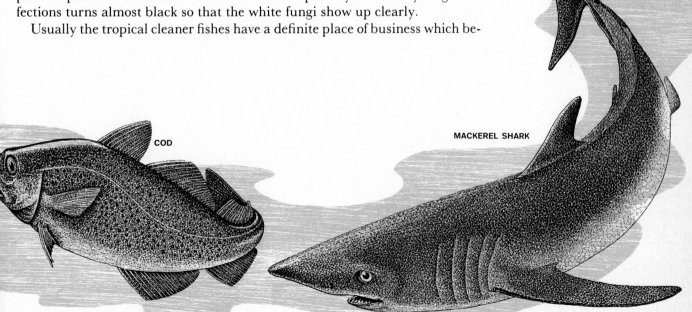

COD

MACKEREL SHARK

comes well known in the community—a distinctive rock or coral head, a patch of white sand, or any other underwater landmark which many fishes are likely to recognize. At these points, there may often be a veritable congestion of customers waiting, more or less impatiently, to be treated for their itches and pains. Limbaugh once counted 300 fish which were handled by a single cleaner during a six-hour period, and noted that a number of individuals returned for additional treatments of infections. He also noted that, besides the normal fish population of the area crowding in to be taken care of, cleaners count among their occasional clientele large fishes, including the huge black sea bass, and pelagic fishes from the open ocean, such as the even larger ocean sunfish.

Another time, to learn what effect the lack of cleaners would have on the fish population, Limbaugh decided to remove all of the cleaner fishes from one station he had been watching in the Bahamas. The results were startling. Within just a few days, the fish population around this once crowded area had dwindled markedly. Within two weeks, there were practically no fish left at all—and those who were still there were in poor shape indeed. Many showed serious infections, including open sores, fungus growths, ragged fins and other evidences of a run-down condition.

WHY more of the customers do not eat the cleaners is a question that still awaits some interesting experimentation. Presumably it is a behavior pattern that has developed through the process of natural selection, just as the cleaners themselves seem to have become specialized for their profession with modified jaws and teeth which are near-perfect instruments for nibbling and probing. Certain it is that in the tropics, where cleaning is so highly developed, the cleaners enjoy extraordinary immunity—in the course of his extensive investigations of California kelpfish, for example, Limbaugh noted that he never once found their favorite cleaner, a small wrasse known as a señorita, in the stomachs of those he dissected. Yet the señorita is the same size as the other fishes on which its customers normally prey.

The most intimate, if least mutually satisfactory relationship of all is that of parasitism. This occurs when one animal or plant lives in or on another, with one getting all the benefit and the other being harmed thereby. The relationship between the parasite and its host may be carried to such extreme lengths that the parasite degenerates almost completely, losing all independent functions except those of reproduction, and even fusing its tissues with those of the host. The host, for its part, may become so debilitated and sapped of its vitality by its unwelcome guest that it dies.

Compared to the total number of fish species, parasitic fishes are not very numerous, but there are some notable examples. One species of pearlfish is a sort of borderline parasite which lives in the body cavity of the sea cucumber, a sausagelike relative of the starfish. An inhabitant of tropical shores, the pearlfish is a slim, transparent creature up to about nine inches long with a thin, pointed tail. It slips into the sea cucumber adroitly tailfirst, through the vent, and in its host's intestines finds not only protection but an occasional meal on the sea cucumber's internal organs. There are other kinds of pearlfish which live in oysters, but the oyster sometimes objects, clamps its shell shut and covers the intruder with a lustrous coat, entombing it forever in a jacket of mother-of-pearl—which explains the fish's name.

Most truly parasitic fishes severely damage their hosts. They are predators in a sense, with the difference that they do not kill their food outright. Lampreys

A PINT-SIZED FREELOADER

A dwarf male anglerfish—about one hundredth as big as the two-to-three-foot-long female—spends its life in parasitic bliss, its jaws fused with the skin tissues of its mate. As an exchange for the nourishment which the female's blood vessels provide, the male acts as a kind of living sperm sac, always on hand to fertilize the eggs.

rasp away the flesh and suck the blood of fishes to which they attach themselves. One of the candirus, a slender little catfish in South American rivers, two or three inches long, enters the gill cavities of a larger kind of catfish. It has sharp teeth and spines on its gill covers with which it lacerates its host, feeding on its flesh. Another, smaller candiru has been known to enter the urinary canals of human bathers, for which reason it is dreaded by the local populations. Once inside the urinary passage the fish begins to suffocate and, in its struggles, erects the spines on its gill covers. The result is agony for the victim and a surgical operation to remove the fish.

But while fishes do not often live as parasites, they themselves are inevitably hosts to a large number of animals which parasitize them. Like almost all other animals, they carry parasites in the intestines, heart, liver, muscles and blood. Among these are many kinds of flatworms, similar to the liver fluke of the sheep, which invade the fishes' digestive tract and blood vessels, as well as tapeworms, roundworms and threadworms. One of the most unusual of all fish parasites is a small, wormlike creature which somehow develops in the eggs of Volga River sturgeon while they are still in the ovary, emerging when the eggs hatch to lead a free-swimming life of its own.

In addition to such internal parasites, fishes are also afflicted with external parasites called fish lice. These are tiny crustaceans which in their larval stage are very much like the larvae of planktonic crustaceans. As adults, some fish lice fix themselves by circular suckers to the outside of the fish, and are able to move about to a certain extent over its body. Others become permanently attached, lose their legs and finally end by looking more like worms than crustaceans. Still others, like ticks, bury their three-pronged heads in the flesh of their hosts. Various fresh-water mussels, in their early stages, parasitize fishes by clamping onto fins or gill filaments and using the fishes for transportation until they have reached maturity, when they let themselves fall off and sink to the bottom.

ALL these relationships, from the most casual associations to parasitism and simple predation, are primarily concerned with food and individual safety. But there are, in the fish's world, other associations which are apparently concerned with collective security between individual fish of the same kind.

Broadly speaking, there are four degrees of social behavior to be distinguished among fishes. There is, first, the solitary fish. Then there are aggregations, in which the fish are assembled randomly in a disoriented crowd, like the cod on their feeding grounds. Next come schools, in which the fish are all lined up with one another with a set swimming distance between them. Still farther up the scale are pods, in which the fish form a dense, close mass, crowding so closely that their bodies are in physical contact.

Although a particular pattern of social behavior tends to be characteristic of each species, more than one social pattern may be observed in any one species, depending on the circumstances and sensory factors involved. A solitary fish may simply be temporarily out of touch, visually or otherwise, with its comrades. Such an individual may school with a different species rather than be alone. Aggregations, which chiefly occur on feeding grounds or spawning grounds or both, appear to depend on the fishes' remaining within sight or sound of each other—and indeed, some species that characteristically aggregate do make considerable noise. Schooling is most frequently observed among the pelagic fishes, especially the herring and its relatives. Here the stability of the school may

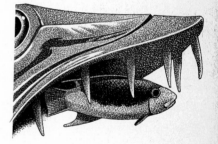

A FAIR EXCHANGE

The wrasse and the barracuda have a relationship beneficial to both known as mutualism. The wrasse, swimming fearlessly among the barracuda's dagger-sharp teeth, helps keep its host infection-free by feeding on bacterial growths in its mouth.

depend upon visual contact, with schools tending to break up during the night to re-form at daybreak. On the other hand, the lateral-line system may play a significant role in schooling, especially in those cases where schools appear to persist after nightfall. Thus herrings kept in a tank form schools only in daylight, breaking up when the light falls below a certain strength, but in the sea they seem to school at night as well as by day.

A big school behaves as though it were a single organism. Its structure is surprisingly regular, with approximately the same number of fish swimming in each of its three dimensions, ahead, beside and on top of each other. On approaching the surface or in shallow water, the school tends to spread out in a layer. In a school of anchovies swimming free between the surface and the bottom, the larger fish are generally underneath and the smaller ones on top. There are definite limits in size in a big school, too—in a school of herring the limit of size difference is about 50 per cent, with no fish in the school more than half again as large or as small as the average size for the school. Any fish above or below the size limit sheer off and form schools among themselves. Occasionally schools break apart, or small schools fuse into larger units.

Although the safety of the group seems to be the primary advantage of the schooling habit, the reaction to the threat of danger appears to be different in different fishes. Herring school closely on the approach of danger, and anchovies under attack by predatory enemies crowd together so closely that they form dense, compact balls. On the other hand, the mackerel of the tropics scatter in all directions and dive when approached by a net.

Another curious manifestation of the schooling habit is that of forming a "mill," or wheel, in which thousands of fish play "follow-the-leader" round and round in a circle. This is perhaps the result of being crowded in a confined space, a small pool or shallow water. There is an old wreck on the bottom outside Zanzibar harbor on the east coast of Africa whose stout steel shell encloses a deep, narrow pool of clear water in which thousands of mullets wheel ceaselessly in dense, compact masses. When approached with a net, the wheel disperses, but it re-forms at once when the net is withdrawn and the fish take up their endless circling again.

To what extent sound plays a part in the formation of schools and the governing of their action is still a subject of interesting experimentation. A great many fishes, notably the jewfish, make audible noises which may be recognition signals for aggregating, and many more make noises inaudible to the human ear. These sounds are of very low frequency, but they can be picked up by sensitive instruments and magnified so that they can be heard. They have been described as "like water pouring," and may be caused by movements of the fishes' musculature or bone structure. They seem to occur mainly when a school is active, moving purposefully or changing direction, and not when it is idling along or at rest.

Scientists at the Bermuda Biological Station found that they could make schools of anchovies and jackfish change direction by playing back these swimming sounds under water. When a sudden loud noise was made under water near the school, the fish nearest to the source of the noise gave a visible start and turned away. This reaction to the noise traveled right through the school, but seemed to communicate itself from fish to fish rather than in the form of actual sound waves, with each fish reacting to the movement of its closest neighbor. Sounds made above the water had no visible effect, nor did distracting actions such as waving arms. On the other hand, if a boat above was rocked, the school instantly changed direction, reacting immediately to the vibrations set up by the rocking action.

Similar experiments to determine the part played by sight showed that blinded fish could not school with a slowly moving school, but instantly took station with them if the school accelerated—at which point the lateral-line system probably became effective. Fish blinded in one eye only were unable to form up on their blind side but could school normally on the side of their good eye.

Probing the role of sight still further, researchers at the Torry Research Station in Aberdeen, Scotland, set movable frames crisscrossed with nylon twine in a tankful of herring. Normally, the fish swam around and around the tank, making a complete circuit every 30 seconds. When the barrier of netting was placed in the tank, the school stayed off to one side of it. Whenever a fish did chance to slip through, it would always make its way back again to return to the school, although it could pass through the barrier only by approaching it at almost a right angle. Clearly, the fish preferred the safety of the school to swimming alone, even if rejoining it involved several efforts to get through the netting. Brightly colored twine, furthermore, proved a more effective barrier than twine which matched the tank walls, indicating that eyesight was an important factor to the school in avoiding obstacles.

Schools appear to form spontaneously and continuously, and in their steady progress through the water they do not follow any leader or set of leaders. Fish traveling in the vanguard often drop back and are replaced by others from the ranks, and when the school changes course, the fish on the flank find themselves on the leading edge, while what was the leading edge becomes a flank. Such a maneuver, even when executed in a large school of a million fish or more, is carried out with such precision that an observer looking down on it from above, as from an airplane, has the impression of watching a single, amoebalike creature flowing through the water in a coordinated, sinuous movement that gives no hint of the tremendous number of individuals involved. It is almost as though there were some central control system governing the entire school.

T HAT there could be no such central control in a mass involving hundreds of thousands of fish is, of course, obvious—yet the question remains: how do the fishes do it? Somewhere in their life history, there must be some factor, some phase of growth, perhaps, which explains the mystery of this highly organized social behavior—but where and what is it?

The biologist Evelyn Shaw, of New York's American Museum of Natural History, went back to the very beginning in a series of experiments aimed at answering these questions. Observations made of two species of the common silverside, a tiny schooling fish abundant in the shore waters of New England, led her to believe that schooling began when the fry, which hatch as larvae about four and a half millimeters (a quarter of an inch) long, had reached a length of 11 to 12 millimeters. But whether schooling began suddenly or developed slowly she was unable to determine, so she took her experiments into the laboratory, with very interesting results.

Working with silversides hatched in a tank from the egg, she found that schooling did develop gradually in a characteristic pattern of fish-to-fish approach and orientation. The first phase, involving the newly hatched fry, came when fry met fry, approached within a quarter of an inch or so, and then darted away. When the fry had reached a length of eight to nine millimeters, they might swim together for a second or two if they met head to tail—that is, with one following the other. If they met head on, however, they would sheer off rapidly as if in fright. Soon, however, the head-to-tail approach would become predominant and the fry would swim together or on parallel courses for as long as five or 10 seconds.

The first signs of consistent schooling appeared when the fry were 10 to 10½ millimeters long, and at this point a characteristic behavior pattern set in. One fry would approach the tail of another and both would briefly vibrate their bodies in a series of rapid motions. The two would then swim off in tandem or parallel to each other, maintaining formation for as long as a minute. Occasionally they might be joined by other fry to form a recognizable, if ragged, little school. At 11 to 12 millimeters, as many as 10 might thus form up, and by the time the fry were 14 millimeters long, they were schooling steadily and with increasing discipline.

Thus it was established that schooling is indeed something which fishes develop gradually, not something they suddenly and inexplicably do. The question still remained: do they require each other's company? Would they school if they were raised individually, in total isolation?

Pursuing this line of inquiry, Dr. Shaw, with some difficulty, succeeded in raising a number of silverside fry in individual tanks so constructed that they had no contact with the outside world whatever, not even with their own reflections, since the tank sides were coated with paraffin. When they reached schooling size, these fry were placed for the first time with others of their species reared together from the same hatch in a normal way. And although they appeared at first confused, bumping into their fellows and sometimes swimming away as though they wished to be alone, the isolated fry were schooling normally within four hours.

Curiously enough, fry that had all been reared in total isolation formed schools within 10 minutes of making each other's acquaintance—far more quickly than if they had been put together with normally reared fry. Others, however, which had been isolated only after they were a week old, took two hours and a half to form schools—from which Dr. Shaw speculated that their early contact with their fellows, at the meet-and-shy-away stage, had set up some blocks against their species-mates which had to be overcome before they would school normally. Very likely, Dr. Shaw concluded, this might simply be due to the fact that their first look at each other frightened them—then, put into individual tanks all by themselves, they never had a chance to get over this initial and frightening impression, and hence were slow to approach each other when reunited in a common tank.

From the tiny silverside swimming in a laboratory tank to the great schools of tuna sweeping their predatory way through shoals of anchovies in the wide Pacific is a long jump—and yet, as other aspects of communal living in the sea have taught us, it is not by any means an illogical one. For in the struggle that goes on continuously beneath the surface of the water, schooling may improve the chances of the species to survive. Schooling behavior means that the tiny fry emerging from aimlessly laid eggs have a way of finding themselves in groups—groups which offer them protection, ease in finding mates and sometimes even food. All in all, it is a more efficient way of surviving than alone. Some 4,000 species of fish long ago adopted the schooling habit, and so far as man can tell, it serves them well.

A DIATOM'S SILICA CASE IS RIBBED AND RAYED FOR STRENGTH. ITS FLUTED SURFACE HELPS THE ORGANISM FLOAT UP NEAR THE SUNLIGHT

A Deadly Game of Eating

Drifting in the plankton meadows of sunlit layers, minute plants like the diatom above furnish the fundamental fodder on which the whole hierarchy of fishes depends. Tiny fry living on the diatoms in turn are food for larger plankton eaters, and these again for bigger and bigger fishes in a mortal game of hide-and-seek, of strange arms and stranger allies, that is illustrated on the following pages.

A LARGEMOUTH BASS plays big daddy and big battleship to a fleet of young it has faithfully fathered from egghood. It does so with such baleful male ferocity that many a heavier-weight foe normally lets it swim past unheeded. Except in spawning season, the bass has small use for the female of its species, chasing her off as soon as the eggs are laid and left under its protection.

TANGLED CLUSTERS OF BASS EGGS AWAIT HATCHING

FIVE-WEEK FINGERLINGS fending for themselves dart about in the underwater jungle. Though still infant bass, they can eat insect larvae and tiny crustaceans in fresh-water plankton.

A BACHELOR BASS at the end of its first year—a year of escapes from many predators, including perhaps its parents and sibling fry—measures about six inches long and swims alone.

Life Story of a Bass

In the many environments in which fishes live— dark abyss or sunny shallow, plankton layer or shelving shore bottom, brackish swamp or upland stream—fresh water, where versatile hunters from the land join the usual predators of the submarine world, has competitive pressures all its own. And in such waters, most anglers agree, few fishes are smarter or more game than the American largemouth bass, shown in intimate detail on these and the following two pages.

Spawning in the quiet waters of eastern North America, largemouth bass show their indomitable will to survive by the fierce protection each male bass gives first to its eggs (above) and then to its hatched fry (opposite). A week or two after hatching, the fry start nibbling at insect larvae and from then on, forsaking their father, they become progressively more formidable as meat-eating hunters in their own right. Their wide mouths grow wider. They terrorize the crappies and bluegills of their own sunfish family and also one another. The luckiest, smartest and strongest of them may go on living, hunting and growing to an age of 20 years, a length of almost three feet and a weight of 25 pounds. Some experts believe they would go on growing forever except that finally the eater is eaten and the killer killed—either by some lowly germ or parasite preying from within or by a superior assailant from another environment like the one on the next page.

A FULL-FLEDGED HUNTER, rounding out two years of age and scaled in the gray-green of an adult bass, now feeds on frogs, one of which it has caught here, crayfish or even baby muskrat.

133

IN FULL CAREER, a strong adult bass rockets from the depths of a stream (*above*) to grab a duckling. Only one webbed foot is seen at center right as the victim vanishes in a froth of bubbles.

IN DESPERATE FLIGHT from a hungry otter (*below*), this bass is swimming for its life from one of the few underwater animals that is bigger, smarter, faster and more voracious than itself.

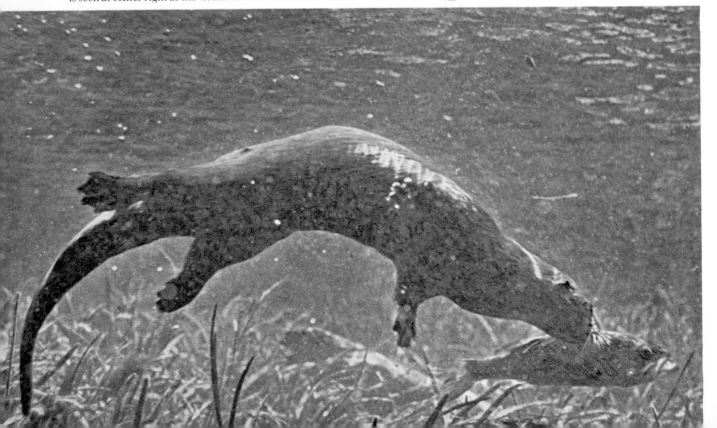

PREDATOR BECOMES PREY as the bass struggles futilely to escape from the otter's sharp teeth. The otter will carry its victim ashore, tease it for a while, and then swallow it down. Thus, in this particular case, the food chain has reached its conclusion —but in life's never-ending cycle it has already begun again as the young of the dying bass begin their predatory careers.

The Finny Art of Camouflage

Bass in a lake or sharks in the ocean grow large enough compared to the foes around them so that they can swim about boldly and rely on offense as the best defense. But smaller fishes must usually be more circumspect. And this they manage by playing dead or depending on camouflage to hide them while a foe goes by—or, conversely, a meal comes within reach. In the variegated underwater seascape, many fishes have long since learned to stick to one home territory to which they are adapted. The elaborate sargassum fish above stays in the shadowy realm of brown weed beds where, perfectly concealed, it can prey on tiny fishes and crustaceans —this in spite of the fact that it can barely swim at all, but stalks about stiltedly on jointed flippers. The equally belligerent scorpion fish, exemplified by the hoary creature opposite above, is attuned to rocky ocean-bottom lands. There it lies about, leaping at unwary prey, fending off attackers with spines so toxic that bathers have died from the stings of some species. By contrast, the timid little shield darter shown opposite below simply hides on its beige stream bed, streaking inconspicuously fast when it moves and lying inconspicuously still at rest.

LIKE AN ALGAE-COVERED ROCK, the scorpion fish, *Scorpaenopsis gibbosa*, lies on the bottom, but when something appetizing comes by it leaps with startling swiftness in pursuit.

IN TANGLED SEAWEED the sargassum fish—three are shown in this photograph—remain invisible to food and foe by being tasseled, knobbed and colored exactly like their environment.

A FRESH-WATER SHIELD DARTER HUNTING FOR MINUTE ORGANISMS ALTERNATELY DARTS AND LIES ON GRAVEL STREAM BEDS ITS OWN COLOR

THE WAVE-PATTERNED UNDULATE TRIGGERFISH ERECTS ITS THREE-SPINED FINNY WEAPON. THE BARBS CAN BE FLIPPED UP OR DOWN

Many-Faceted Protection

The gentle art of disappearing into the woodwork is at best a passive way to survive, even for fishes like the little French grunt opposite, which can adjust its disguise at will for different settings. Most fishes, however, have more tangible accessories in their arsenal of survival. Porcupinefish prickle their way through. Puffers bluff it. Electric eels shock, flyingfish escape into another medium and many gobies go underground. The little pearlfish exploits a skeleton-key slimness to steal into other animals' insides. The peaceable plant-eating surgeonfish surprises meat-eating molesters with a small, razor-sharp pair of switch blades on the sides of its tail which snap open in emergencies and often scar the hands of unknowing fishermen. The clingfish is favored with a powerful holdfast sucker, with which it moors itself firmly to rocks in tidal pools, resisting would-be predators and feeding on hapless crustaceans which are washed into its jaws.

The triggerfish above, one of 30-odd species all armed the same way, has its first three dorsal fin spines modified into a bizarre weapon. The first spine on the front of the fin cocks the weapon, the second releases it so that it can be raised up in a prickly barb or be bowed down flat. Defensively, the spine may serve as an active deterrent to fishes attempting to swallow the triggerfish, and also as a hook to wedge it more obstinately in the coral-reef crannies where it hides. Like so many mysteries of the ocean, this reveals the elaborate lengths to which fish adaptation has gone and the great gulfs in knowledge for future skin divers to fill.

BY DAY the French grunt, also called a ronco, or snorer, because of noises it makes, dawdles and drowses in West Indian waters, adapting to the seascape with sunny, shadow-striped yellows.

BY NIGHT the French grunt turns tawny and gray, cloaking itself in dark-phase coloration to stalk small fishes and crustaceans. A pint-sized predator, it averages seven inches in length.

THE CLINGFISH anchors itself with the powerful holdfast organ on its underside. Its sucker, unlike that of the gobies, is constructed from the pectoral as well as the pelvic fins.

THE SURGEONFISH opens a yellow jackknife device on each side of its tail. The blade was evolved from a scale and is so attached that the fish can snap it open or flatten it shut.

THE PEARLFISH, some six inches long, swims in search of a host. Supple and slim, it can slither inside the intestine of some invertebrate animal for protection or parasitic feeding.

A SEA CUCUMBER, a relative of the starfish, plays host to the pearlfish that peers out of the sea cucumber's body. Small pearlfish sometimes wind up as pearls in victimized oysters.

A HERD OF GRAY-BLUE GOATFISH, WAITING TO BE CLEANED, HOVERS AROUND TWO BUTTERFLYFISH. THE ROUND FLAT BUTTERFLIES USE THEIR MA

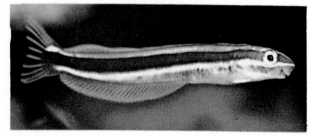

A PHONY CLEANER is *Aspidontus rhinorhynchus*. It looks like just another striped wrasse, a dependable fish cleaner, but when a parasite-laden sufferer swims up, *Aspidontus* takes a big bite.

Friendly Cleaners

Big predators against which a fish can arm or take refuge add up to only half its roster of foes. There are also minute crustaceans, worms and bacteria ever ready to infest its scales, gill slits and orifices, killing it far more commonly than sharks do. To get rid of these parasites, most fishes depend on the services of certain shrimps and smaller fishes, like the wrasses opposite. The cleaners eat off the

DOCTORING A SURGEONFISH, a striped wrasse known as the lipfish goes over the skin, gnawing off bacteria and crustaceans and gently nibbling at wounds caused by bacterial infections.

HEALING AN EEL of the malevolent moray family, a Hawaiian rainbow wrasse works its way up along the neck. The eel is a fairly safe patient, though it sometimes eats cleaner shrimps.

A SPOTTED TRUNKFISH, also called a boxfish (*below*), sometimes exudes a poison that deters aggressors, but here it withholds its toxins while a lipfish wrasse gives it a going-over.

MALL BUCK TEETH NOT ONLY TO CLEAN, BUT ALSO TO SCAVENGE ROCKS

incrustations and the cleansed submit to being scavenged. In temperate waters, to be sure, where the relationship of cleaner and cleaned is less highly developed, the daredevil cleaners are more likely to end up in their clients' stomachs. But in the tropics they safely advertise themselves in bright colors, service whole queues of waiting fishes and are even mimicked by fierce fakes like the blenny at left.

THE TOXIC TENTACLES of a sea anemone provide a damselfish with a safe domicile. It lays its eggs in the poisonous shelter of the anemone's base and sometimes even rubs up against the tentacles like a cat. The secret of this little intruder's immunity may be a mucous secretion that protects it from the anemone's explosive sting cells, or it may be simply acquired immunity.

WASHED AGAINST A SHORE-ANCHORED STARFISH, AN OCEAN-GOING HERRING IS HELPLESSLY TRAPPED IN THE SEDENTARY PREDATOR'S GRASP

Unfriendly Tentacles

The relationship between fishes and invertebrate animals of the submarine environment is, for the most part, one of predator and prey, with the fishes usually playing the predator's role. Mollusks, crustaceans, arthropods and soft-bodied creatures of all kinds fall victim to the fishes' appetites, and what defenses the invertebrates have are usually of a passive kind. But some of the sea's soft-bodied animals do have weapons of their own, and among these one which the fishes have the most reason to fear is the tentacle. The echinoderm starfish entraps a stranded herring (*above*) and the flowerlike sea anemone of the coelenterates poisons just about every kind of fish that brushes against it. However, some damselfishes seem entirely immune to anemone stings and often hide among the tentacles for protection.

A SEA ANEMONE TRAPS A FISH IN ITS ARMS AND STINGS IT TO DEATH

USING ITS LONG TENTACLES, IT DRAWS A VICTIM TO ITS MOUTH

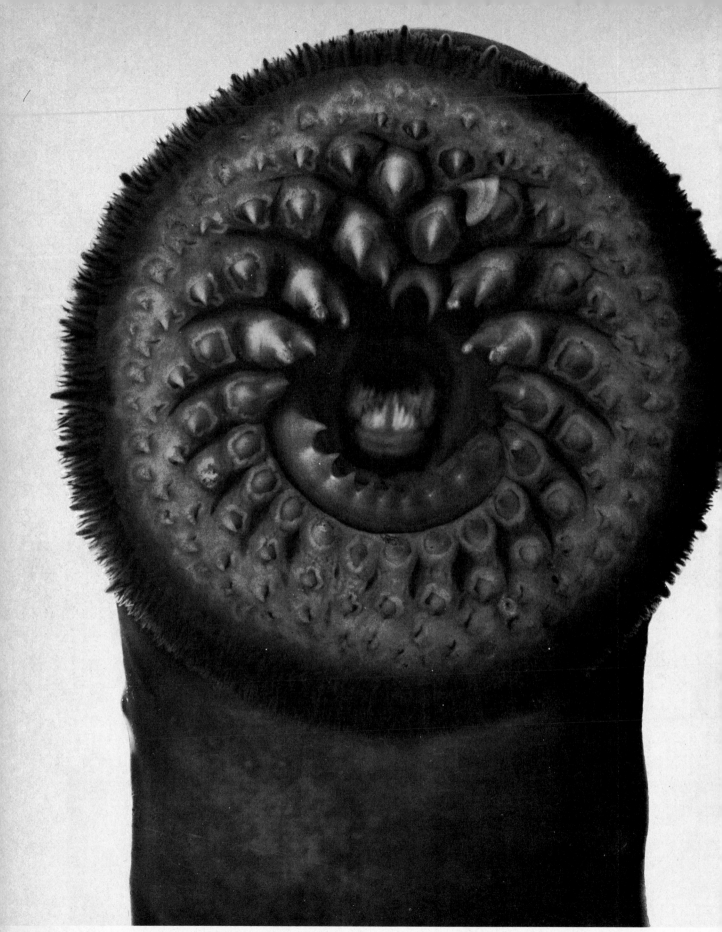

A SEA LAMPREY'S SUCKING MOUTH contains up to 125 sharp teeth with which, rasping and drilling back and forth, it cuts through the scales of other fishes. Back in the lamprey's mouth, glands exude an anticoagulant which keeps the victims' blood flowing. The sucker is also used as a holdfast when the lamprey goes from the ocean along fresh-water streams to spawn.

Some Most Unusual Predators

It is the normal lot of a fish, in the ceaseless game of hunt and eat, eventually to be devoured by some creature bigger than it. However, two forms of predation shown on these and the pages that follow take a different turn—one a lingering death by bloodletting, the other a surprise attack from above.

The sea lamprey long ago organized its way of life along lines that seem to humans to be unpleasant, but which for the lampreys are highly effective. The lamprey line dates back some 400 million years, when fishes already had achieved mobility and developed cartilage backbones but had as yet no jaws to bite with. The lampreys have perfected a sucker to latch onto other fishes, scrape open a wound and bleed out a living. The effectiveness of this instrument even today has been brought home to Americans with the opening of the Welland Canal around Niagara Falls. Sea lampreys promptly began using the canal to make their way into the Great Lakes, and since then they have exploited their ancient weapon so well against the fishes in the lakes that only recently has man begun to succeed in arresting their depredations short of actual extermination of native species.

Less dramatic, but in the long run more important, is the constant attrition of small fishes by birds. To see an example of how one bird catches a free-swimming fish in the water, turn the page.

THE DEATH LOCK of a lamprey on a lake trout is demonstrated by biologist Vernon C. Applegate. The lake trout, along with several other species of fishes, has been almost wiped out all over the Great Lakes area.

THE SEEDS OF DESTRUCTION are counted in the egg-filled body of a 15-inch female lamprey. There are over 50,000 of them, each a threat to any fish in the Atlantic or in any of its tributary streams and lakes.

PLUNGING STRAIGHT DOWNWARD, the puffin strikes the herring before it can take evasive action. Underwater, this big bird swims with amazing speed, pumping its wings in rapid strokes.

Having seized the herring, this puffin will probably eat it on the spot; in the wild it might take it to its young, waiting in the deep cliffside burrow in which puffins make their home.

A SCHOOL OF TARPON, gleaming like a wall of silver, glides through Florida Bay. Migrating northward in springtime, this spectacular game fish appears off both Florida coasts and westward along the Gulf Coast.

7

Charting the Great Migrations

MANY fishes are constantly on the move. Others, like most of the species that live in coral reefs, have a particular niche or hole to which they may retire regularly. Still others, including many in fresh water, have well-defined areas, or territories, which they patrol and sometimes even zealously guard against all comers. Many, however, drift about their environment following a general pattern of instinctive seasonal movements. As might be expected, pelagic ocean fishes wander great distances through their featureless environment, guided by temperatures, currents and concentrations of food organisms. On the other hand, some migrations are so specifically oriented as to defy man's ability to explain how the travels are accomplished.

Migratory behavior is fundamentally seasonal, as many fishes seek out the best spawning grounds and later the best food sources, urged on by changes in temperature and a concomitant change in abundance and type of food available. In winter many fresh-water species stop feeding and retire to deeper levels where temperatures are warmer than on the frozen surface. Some, like the bullhead, settle into the mud. On the continental shelves, there are groups of summer and winter species. The summer inshore, or warmer-water species, such as the scup, silver hake and fluke, go out to the edge of the shelf during the winter, where the water temperatures are usually comparatively warm. The winter, or colder-water, species, such as the ocean pout and the long-horned sculpin, come inshore in the winter and go offshore in the summer. Along the eastern coast of the United States a general tendency has been observed for the older and bigger fish of several species to drift toward the north. Some species, especially those of the cod and hake families, occupy different areas during different periods of their life, their movements presumably influenced by the amount of food available and the necessity of reducing cannibalism.

SINCE so many commercially important marine fishes do migrate to a considerable degree, it is interesting to note the apparently strongly developed homesteading characteristics of the redfish. This species normally occurs in very deep water and, of course, cannot be easily studied. Knowledge about its movements has been virtually impossible to obtain. Since it has a gas bladder it cannot be brought to the surface without severe damage or death resulting. On the basis of the distribution of its parasites, however, fishery scientists have deduced that it does not move about much. There is one coastal area in Maine where redfish do occur, most unusually, in shallow water. One of the fishery scientists at the Bureau of Commercial Fisheries Biological Laboratory at Woods Hole set about studying their habits. After appropriately marking these fish so that they could be identified later, he made repeated visits for many years. Individual fish were demonstrated to stay in exactly the same place, give or take a few feet, for periods of as long as five years.

But in northern waters such stay-at-home habits are rare. Fishes journey to their spawning grounds, in some cases to their nursery grounds and sometimes to special feeding grounds. The distances these migrations cover may vary, from mere shifts of depth from inshore to offshore water and back again, to ocean-wide wanderings covering thousands of miles.

Journeys to feeding grounds are usually less regular and ordered than those to spawning grounds, as one might expect since feeding migrations are conditioned at least in part by the amount and distribution of the food, which may change from season to season.

As a general rule, fishes with pelagic eggs make a passive journey, as developing eggs and young fry drift with the plankton away from the spawning grounds. But as grown fish they make an active migration back to the spawning area.

FISH TAGS

The plastic tag seen here on a haddock has an anchor which is inserted under the skin through a small scalpel incision. The capsule, connected by a chain, has a paper roll in it containing coded information. The Atkins tag, shown on a silver hake, is a flat plate attached to a wire or tube that pierces the dorsal muscles and is looped into a figure-eight knot. The tube allows the tag to trail behind the fish. The Peterson tag, the most widely used, consists of two tags skewered by a pin. As seen on the flounder, the pin pierces muscular tissue, its head holding a disk against the skin. A second disk is then slid on the far side and secured by bending the pin point.

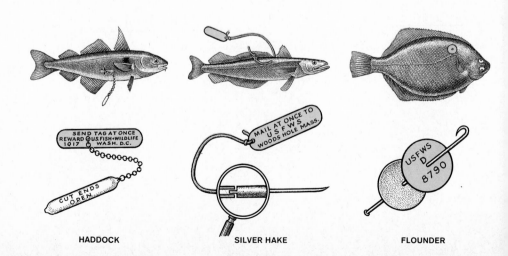

HADDOCK   **SILVER HAKE**   **FLOUNDER**

Plaice eggs shed at the northern end of the English Channel drift northeast and the young fish are scattered on several nursery grounds along the Dutch and German coasts. They make many minor and random movements to special feeding grounds, depending on the abundance and distribution of the larval mollusks, crustaceans and other creatures they seek as food. But in general they move out into deeper water as they grow older. They tend to sort themselves out on the bottom strictly according to size and depth, the deeper the water the bigger the fish. When they mature, the fish unerringly and at the proper time swim back to the spawning grounds near the English Channel.

Similarly the Pacific halibut spawns in the Gulf of Alaska on the continental slope near Kodiak Island in depths of 100 to 150 fathoms. This island lies on the western limb of a great counterclockwise stream around the gulf which carries the halibut fry toward the coast of British Columbia, where the young settle down on the slope. When they grow up they continue along the slope, swimming with the current back to the spawning area near Kodiak Island.

The migrations of the cod are relatively limited in range but regular and seasonal. Cod move to their spawning grounds in the spring, for the first time when about five years old. When they leave the plankton as youngsters, in late summer or fall, they seek the bottom on nursery grounds in rather shallow water, down to about 40 fathoms. As they grow they move out to deeper water for feeding. When the time comes to spawn, they return to the place where they were spawned, returning annually thereafter for as long as they live.

THE spawning cod that support the ancient Norwegian fishery around the Lofoten Islands undertake a considerable migration. The eggs, larvae and young cod tend to drift passively north with the currents, eventually arriving on the Bear Island grounds near Spitsbergen. During their juvenile years they move about from place to place, apparently never going very far. With the onset of maturity, however, they return to the Lofoten Islands spawning area.

Some cod populations mingle on the nursery and feeding grounds, but separate later and go to quite different spawning grounds. Such is the case with the cod that spend the summers off Cape Cod. Some of them spawn off the New Jersey coast while the rest spawn in the Gulf of Maine. There is little or no evidence available to suggest that any appreciable exchange takes place between these spawning groups.

These movements of our northern food fishes are parochial compared with the

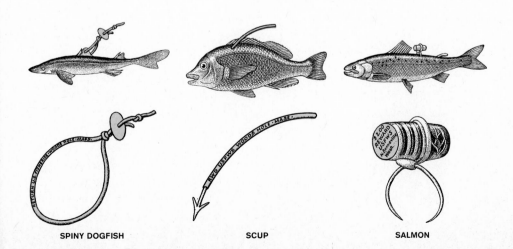

SPINY DOGFISH   **SCUP**   **SALMON**

The "spaghetti" tag used on a spiny dogfish is simply a long plastic tube. It is drawn through the dorsal fin by a removable stainless-steel needle and the two ends are tied together. Sometimes a disk like the one shown is added, but often the information is printed directly on the tube. The flexible "dart" tag worn by the scup is similar, but it is attached by a barbed hook and does not pass through the fin. The sonic tag, shown on a salmon, is the newest innovation. A miniature transmitter which clasps the back muscles by means of tongs, it helps to track the fish over short distances of up to 800 feet. Its batteries have a life of only 100 hours.

far-ranging wanderings of the big predatory pelagic fishes, the bluefin and yellowfin tuna, the albacore and others. Most of these fishes, browsing on the shoals of small plankton-feeding fishes, travel north and south with the summer advance and winter retreat of the warm water.

The bluefin tuna is widespread over the North Atlantic, but it is less abundant and smaller in the Pacific. On the American side of the Atlantic it is believed to have a spawning ground in warm subtropical waters somewhere east of the Bahamas. In May and June of each year, schools of bluefin tuna follow the outer side of the Gulf Stream northward in a great procession through the Florida Strait, passing to feeding grounds among the herring and mackerel off Newfoundland and Nova Scotia. The bluefin is never seen returning by this route, and how it gets back to its tropical ocean hide-out is still a mystery.

On the European side of the Atlantic the bluefin is believed to have a spawning ground near the Azores and travels north as far as the Arctic Circle in the summer months. It has another spawning ground in the Mediterranean.

In the 1920s an Italian zoologist, Massimo Sella, in an early venture into the science of tagging fishes, made a study of the migration of the bluefin from the hooks found in the mouths of fish in various parts of the world. He found fish caught in the Mediterranean that had Portuguese hooks from the Azores, and fish caught off the coast of Spain with hooks from Norway. In Norway the bluefin is sometimes hunted with harpoons, and the harpoons have been recovered from fish caught in the Mediterranean. Off Sardinia a bluefin was caught carrying, embedded in its flesh, a hook of an old discontinued model manufactured in Akron, Ohio. This suggested that there may be a connection between the bluefin of the American side and that of the European side of the Atlantic. Much later, in fact, two bluefin, tagged in July 1954 off Martha's Vineyard, Massachusetts, were recovered five years later in the Bay of Biscay, thus proving that at least some American bluefin do move across to Europe.

These long-distance records for the bluefin have been broken by a long-finned cousin, the albacore. In August 1952, the California Department of Fish and Game tagged 215 albacore just off Los Angeles; nearly 11 months later, one of them was recaptured by a Japanese longline boat 550 miles southeast of Tokyo. It had traveled 4,900 miles in that time. In 1956 an albacore was taken 2,670 miles from its release point, and another was caught over 2,000 miles away.

Massimo Sella's work, however, done over 35 years ago, was that of a pioneer. It gave rise to a line of research which has become of immense importance all over the world. This is the method of tracing the movements of fishes by tagging or marking them. If sufficient tags are returned, the fisheries biologists will have a clue to the movements and migrations of the fishes.

Analysis of tag returns often reveals unexpected as well as useful facts. It may indicate that there is intermingling between seemingly separate populations in different parts of the ocean, or that there are actually separate and distinct stocks where only one was suspected before. The length of the fish is noted when it is tagged and again when it is recaptured, so the biologist will have a measure of its growth rate. Similarly a few scales may have been collected when the fish was tagged for comparison with scales taken when, hopefully, the fish is recaptured. A comparison of such scales makes it possible to verify scale age reading techniques. The number of tags recovered in a given time will provide information on the death rate, or mortality, of the population caused by fishing, after all the risks of tags being lost have been duly assessed and allowed for.

Early attempts at tagging were not very successful and it took a long time to evolve suitable tags which would stay in the fish and not kill or harm it. Fish tags today range from simple pins to sophisticated sonic transmitters. A typical tag is a disk of plastic, clipped like a cuff link with a stainless steel pin through the back muscles of the fish. In the big-scale tuna-tagging experiments in the Pacific and Atlantic, two other types of tag have come into use. One is the "dart" tag, a piece of plastic tubing six or seven inches long, with a nylon dart head which is thrust into the back muscles of the fish. The other, the so-called "spaghetti" tag, is a loop of plastic tubing with the number and date printed on a length of finer tubing running through it. The tube is passed through the back muscles of the fish and the ends of the thread firmly tied.

A most skillfully engineered tag which points the way to methods of fish-following never before possible has been developed by Minneapolis-Honeywell and government scientists for the purpose of tracking salmon. It is a small sonic transmitter, encased in a plastic container and clamped to the back of the fish. Once attached, the transmitter automatically begins to send ultrasonic waves in all directions through the water, and continues to do so for up to 100 hours. With an effective range of 800 feet, the transmissions are easily followed from a boat, and the course of the fish charted as it moves upstream.

Although the early results of the sonic tag have not yet led to any specific conclusions about the behavior of salmon in general, they did prove the feasibility of such advanced scientific methods. The tag itself, with transmitter and batteries, proved to be virtually weightless in water and many fish showed no reaction to it at all. The transmissions, picked up and projected as light blips on a cathode-ray screen, enabled the scientists to track and record all the various movements of the fish with great accuracy, revealing, among other things, a tendency among the salmon to avoid deep water and stick close to the shoreline and to slow down or stop entirely when darkness fell. In the initial experiment, 39 Columbia River salmon and four steelhead trout were successfully followed.

Undamaged fish are always chosen for tagging, handled as carefully as possible so as not to rub any scales off accidentally, and returned to the sea as soon and as gently as possible. Schooling fishes like herrings and sardines are especially difficult to deal with because they are so easily injured.

A PARTICULARLY ingenious method was developed by the California Department of Fish and Game for the tagging of Pacific sardines in a great tagging campaign in the years before the war. The fishermen delivered their catch in bulk to fish-meal plants and thus there was no opportunity for anyone to spot tags. Accordingly the fish were marked by means of small numbered nickel-plated tags slipped into the body cavity with forceps after making a small slit with a scalpel, or else shot into the body cavity with a small pneumatic pistol. The slight wound thus caused soon healed over. In the fish-meal plants, the meal, after drying, passed through hoppers to the grinders. Electromagnets were placed in the hoppers which picked up the tags as they passed by. Altogether between 123,000 and 124,000 sardines were tagged in this way between 1937 and 1942 when the war put an end to the experiment. Four per cent, or somewhat over 5,200 of the tags, had been recovered before the experiment finished.

This campaign showed that the Pacific sardine, from its spawning ground about 50 miles off San Diego, moved inshore up the coast as far as Vancouver Island, while fish tagged by the Canadian, Washington and Oregon governments were found to have moved south to California. It took about six months for a large sardine to move from California to British Columbia, while smaller ones took several years to make the same journey.

A more recent modification of the herring-tagging technique by Bureau of Commercial Fisheries scientists involves the use of a low-level radioactive tag. The tag is not dangerous to fish or man. However, it makes possible the engineering of machinery capable of separating individual fish carrying such tags. This is done while the conveyor belts are carrying the fish into the plant from the fishing boats, without interrupting the unloading operation.

Most commercial fishermen nowadays cooperate readily in returning tags, since they understand how valuable the information will be to them. In the open ocean, where the chances of the fish being caught before it loses the tag or is itself eaten by something else are fairly remote, the proportion of tags returned is usually small, as low as 2 per cent, seldom higher than 30 per cent. For this reason, many years of work are needed before tagging yields positive evidence on the movements of the great wanderers of the open seas.

MIGRATION OF EELS

When the fresh-water eels of North America and Europe are between five and eight years old, they make a remarkable journey to the Sargasso Sea, a huge area of floating seaweed in the Atlantic Ocean between the West Indies and the Azores, where they spawn and die. When the eggs hatch, the fry begin the hazardous return trip to their respective coastal streams. American eels take a year to reach their destination and are miniature adults when they arrive. But European eels take three times as long to cross the Atlantic and arrive in the same state of development as the American ones.

RESEARCH scientists spend a great deal of time and effort in tagging a wide variety of fish species. To encourage the greatest possible cooperation, rewards are usually paid for the return of the tags. Research of this kind is difficult even under the best of conditions. The tag may be missed by the fishermen, and be found later on after the fish has been shipped to market far from the port of landing. Even if the tag is found by the local supermarket or by a customer who is preparing the fish at home, it is of value to the scientists who tagged it, and therefore well worth the slight trouble of mailing it to the address marked on the tag. A great deal of effort is sometimes spent tracking down the vessel that landed the fish in the hopes of determining where the fish was caught. The following few examples illustrate the extensive tagging efforts undertaken by various marine fishery laboratories.

Marine biologists at Woods Hole tagged nearly 70,000 fish, including many ground-fish species, during the five-year period of 1956 to 1960, recovering nearly 17 per cent of the cod, 10 per cent of the haddock, 8 per cent of the scup and 28 per cent of the yellowtail flounders tagged. Scientists at the Lowestoft laboratory on the east coast of England marked 19,000 fishes between 1929 and 1932 in the southern North Sea. By 1936, some 7,000, or 37 per cent, of the tags had been returned. Research personnel of the Fisheries Research Institute of the University of Washington have tagged more than 78,000 salmon on the high seas through 1961 and recovered nearly 4 per cent.

The Inter-American Tropical Tuna Commission, with its headquarters at the Scripps Institution of Oceanography, La Jolla, California, had by the end of 1960 tagged 24,755 yellowfins and 58,558 skipjacks and recovered respectively 5.6 per cent and 2.6 per cent of the tags.

There are many species of fish which go from the sea to fresh water to spawn, and the voyages they make range from those of the striped bass and the shad, which live close to shore and move upriver some distance, to those of the salmon, which lives normally as an adult in the sea far from land, but always returns to its birthplace in some far inland stream.

One can never safely generalize about fishes. There are always contradictions, and one of the oddest is the case, which came to light in recent years, of the striped bass, the sporting fish which revolutionized the economy of the Santee-Cooper Lake basin in South Carolina. There, in a perfectly natural and strictly unintentional way, man accomplished with the striped bass what he had never before succeeded in doing: he adapted this fish to fresh water.

The striped bass, known as the rockfish south of the Mason-Dixon Line, is a seasonal migratory fish native to the East Coast of North America. It normally comes into brackish or fresh water to spawn; after hatching, the fry slowly work their way downriver and out to sea again. Striped bass were transplanted 50 years ago with good success to California, but all efforts to plant this fine sporting fish in fresh water met with failure—until the Santee-Cooper Hydroelectric and Navigation Project, an inspiration born in Depression years to bring cheap power and new industry to hard-hit South Carolina, was completed in November 1941.

At that time the bass which in the normal course of events came up the Santee and Cooper Rivers to spawn, found their way back to the sea blocked by two great dams. Behind these dams the river waters backed up to form two sizable bodies of water, Lake Marion and Lake Moultrie. A navigation lock in the Pinopolis dam at Lake Moultrie still permitted occasional access to the lower reaches of the Cooper and the sea beyond, and doubtless some bass escaped down it, while others came up through into the lake. In the main, however, the bass were penned up in fresh water—and oddly enough, they thrived on it. By the late 1950s so many were being caught that sport fishing in the Santee-Cooper area was a multimillion-dollar business.

The migratory instincts of these landlocked striped bass have also become adapted to their new habitat. Instead of going from the sea to fresh-water rivers to spawn, they now go from the lakes up the Congaree and Wateree Rivers, and the returning fry find in the shallow waters of the reservoirs all the food they need. The adult bass, for their part, have found in the gizzard shad, a freshwater relative of the herring they would be feeding on in the ocean, a perfect substitute for their salt-water food.

T HE Santee-Cooper stripers are the most recent examples of salt-water fish that have become landlocked, but by no means the only ones. On both sides of the American continent, there are salmon which live always in fresh water and never go to sea at all. Behaving more typically, king salmon, from the Salmon River, Idaho, travel as far west as the central Aleutian Islands before returning 2,500 miles to ascend the Columbia and Snake Rivers to their home spawning grounds. Red, or sockeye, salmon travel over halfway to Asia from their lakes in British Columbia, and chum salmon from southeast Alaska may make a round trip of 3,500 miles to the central Aleutians in search of food. Salmon on the Asiatic side as well travel great distances out to sea, ranging as far eastward as the central Aleutians, a length of at least 1,000 miles.

On the European side of the Atlantic Ocean, salmon have been caught at widely scattered points, and fish tagged in Scotland have been recovered in trawls as far away as Greenland, Norway and Iceland. They too make ocean voyages of great length, and one theory is that they follow the courses of old rivers out across the continental shelf, as in the case of the Rhine, whose ancient bed continues on beneath the North Sea to open into the abyss between the Orkneys and Norway.

Fisheries research literature is replete with observation and speculation about the manner in which salmon return from the high seas. It has been variously suggested that they follow currents, guide themselves by the sun using polarized light like bees, even use sights on the stars, or perhaps have a directional memory. None of these suggestions is necessarily foolish although some needlessly

TRANSFORMATION OF AMERICAN EELS

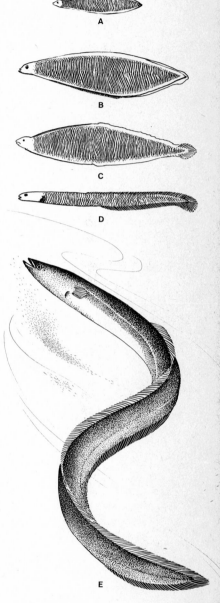

While little is known about exactly where and how eels deposit their eggs, scientists have learned much about their development after hatching by netting the larvae and examining them along their migratory paths. After hatching in winter or early spring, the transparent, relatively broad, leaf-thin larvae are known as leptocephali (A, B, C). Within 12 months they develop into rounded, three-inch, transitional creatures called elvers (D). The elvers closely resemble the adults, which at times reach four feet in length (E).

strain one's credulity. Research of this kind is exceedingly difficult to carry out and may well continue for many years. A University of Rhode Island scientist has developed a provocative new theory, using an electronic computer to perform the tedious calculations required. His findings strongly suggest that salmon may actually have only a minimum of the directional, or navigational, sense they have always been credited with. Actually, according to this theory, they may swim quite randomly on their return—but such are their numbers that enough of them always will hit the general vicinity of their parent river to complete the spawning run. The computer calculations appeared to prove out with actual experience to an impressive degree—they showed, for example, that the number of salmon actually returning is equal to the number which, on the basis of experience, could be expected to return from a given spawning run.

OTHER researchers, however, give different answers, which suggest that the salmon actually knows what it is doing. One team headed by a University of Wisconsin zoologist, Arthur D. Hasler, made a detailed study of the homing salmon, both in the stream phase and open-sea phase, and developed the theory that downstream migration is a passive movement depending on currents and feeding grounds. Most salmon species, both in the Pacific and the Atlantic, stay at their deep-sea feeding grounds for two or three years until sexual maturity somehow signals for their return. Then the fish begin "one of the most remarkable journeys to be found in the animal kingdom," as Hasler puts it. In the open sea, neither water nor the ocean bottom can conceivably furnish any landmark to the salmon. Its most likely navigational aid is the position of the sun. The ability to use this sun-compass for open-sea navigation has definitely been established in some other species of fish. So far, because of the great distances over which the salmon travels, no direct test has been feasible.

Such navigation by celestial cues would be capable of bringing the salmon to within 50 miles of the home coastline. There, another remarkable mechanism takes over. Before leaving for the open sea the young salmon is imprinted with an olfactory "image" of its home water, based on the water's chemical characteristics. Once the salmon finds itself back at the home coast, it can sniff its way back to its ancestral stream, rejecting every tributary that does not bear the exact home odor.

Although the hypothesis of sun-compass navigation is arguable, since it does not explain how the salmon travels at night, the theory that the salmon is being led by its nose all the way back to its birthplace is supported by other findings. A University of Washington team in Seattle has reported that by using electroencephalographs on salmon in laboratory tests, it was discovered that water from the home stream of the fish produces vigorous responses, while water from elsewhere does not. Other scientists in the same university found that by injecting memory-blocking chemicals into homing salmon, recognition of home water was largely lost.

If a salmon finds its native river blocked, it may go up a neighboring one and start a new spawning run as a result. Many of our rivers nowadays have become effectively blocked to the spawning runs of salmon by man-made hazards such as hydroelectric dams and river pollution. However, it takes quite a lot to stop a salmon on its way to its spawning ground. Salmon going upstream are said to travel at a speed of six or seven miles per hour, and the habit which both salmon and trout have of leaping up waterfalls is well known and most spectacular. They leap heights of 8 to 10 feet at a clip and, if they do not at first succeed, go on trying until they either do succeed or fall back exhausted.

Salmon traveling to spawn do not feed and become steadily thinner and weaker. Indeed the king, or Chinook, salmon, on its journey to its spawning ground thousands of miles up the Yukon, may fail to complete the journey and die. Nevertheless, as every fisherman knows, Atlantic salmon running upstream will snap at flies, but this may be a mere feeding reflex and it has been suggested that salmon go for flies which look most like the crustaceans they feed on in the sea.

A group of biologists and medical scientists, intrigued by the spectacularly rapid aging of spawning salmon, found that as soon as the salmon returns to fresh water its pituitary gland goes out of control and in a couple of weeks the salmon ages as much as a man does in 30 years. Within that brief period of time this sparkling, beautiful creature degenerates into a senile fish with peeling skin and a disintegrating nervous system. Is this "programmed death" inherent in the genetic makeup of the salmon, or is it triggered by its return to fresh water? Answers to such questions are being sought by scientists who hope that they may help man to delay old age and senility.

What urge compels salmon to travel upstream, leaping waterfalls and exposing themselves to many predators, only to die when spawning is done? It is generally supposed that they are returning to ancestral spawning grounds, that their original home was only in fresh water and their migration out to sea a secondarily acquired feeding journey.

Many fishes other than the salmon go upriver to spawn. The cisco and the char, both related to the salmon, are typically anadromous, and both have landlocked relatives. Various members of the herring family, such as the shad and alewife, spawn in many of the rivers along the east coast of the United States. The sea lamprey also spawns in fresh water. The species has fully adapted itself to fresh water in the Great Lakes, where it is presently an unmitigated pest because of its attacks on lake fish.

The catadromous fishes spend their youth in fresh water but travel out to sea to spawn, reversing the life history of the salmon, alewife and sea lamprey. There are not nearly so many of them as there are of the anadromous fishes, and the best known is the common eel. In the Southern Hemisphere there are some small fish, called smelts in the Falkland Islands and, when young, whitebait in New Zealand, which run down the streams and spawn in schools in the surf.

THE tracking-down of the spawning area of the fresh-water eel is a saga of marine biology and loses nothing of its wonder for having been told so often.

Until the end of the 18th Century no one had ever seen a fresh-water eel with sex glands developed at all. From earliest times, therefore, it had been supposed that eels were spontaneously generated out of mud. Then, in the 17th Century, it was noted in Italy that adult eels went down to the sea and young ones came up out of it into fresh water. In 1856 a German scientist described a flat, transparent creature which he had caught in the Strait of Messina. He did not recognize it as having anything to do with eels and named it *Leptocephalus brevirostris* (short-snouted thinhead). In 1896 two Italian scientists discovered that this was the larva of the eel. They too worked in the Strait of Messina, where tide rips cast up plankton in masses on the shore, and by examining hundreds of stranded leptocephali they were able to establish beyond doubt that they were anatomically related to the grown eel.

At the beginning of the present century, Danish research ships, looking for young cod and eggs in the North Atlantic, found leptocephalus larvae in hundreds in the open ocean. A young Danish marine biologist, Johannes Schmidt, began an intensive search with fine-meshed nets towed by Danish ships at various depths all over the North Atlantic Ocean. He searched through hundreds of hauls and found that he could draw up a chart showing that the leptocephali became progressively smaller and smaller in size as one approached the Sargasso Sea, where the smallest larvae of all were found.

The conclusion Schmidt drew from this was that the European and American fresh water eels spawned in the Sargasso Sea in depths of about 200 fathoms. Further study has shown that the American eel has a spawning area slightly to the west of that of the European eel, nearer to the American coast.

Leptocephali hatch in the spring and drift northward with the Gulf Stream. The American larvae have a shorter larval youth than the European larvae, and arrive the following winter on the east coast of the United States. The European larvae drift far north in the Gulf Stream and have a much longer larval period. It corresponds with the time it takes them to drift to the coast of Europe, some two and a half to three years. In the spring on both coasts, but two years later on the European than on the American coast, the leptocephali lose their flattened, ribbonlike shape and become rounded elvers or "glass" eels about three inches long. They then migrate upriver to distant ponds and streams, sometimes in enormous swarms. In the Severn River in England these swarms are known as eelfares, and they are caught in nets in vast quantities.

Eels have been observed leaving their rivers and ponds in late summer and early fall, making their way downstream to the sea. From a yellowish sheen, they change to silver, and in the fall apparently begin the long journey to the Sargasso Sea. When the yellow eel has become a silver eel and taken to the sea, its gut degenerates so that, like the salmon and the lamprey, it cannot feed during its long arduous migration to its far-off spawning ground.

THERE have been doubts about the migration of the European eel to the Sargasso Sea. One expert has suggested that only the American eels actually get there, and that the eggs which hatch in the westerly waters of the Sargasso Sea drift northwest to become American eels, while those which hatch in the water to the eastward drift northeast and become European eels. The principal difference between the European and American eels is a consistent difference in the number of vertebrae—the European eel has about 115 and the American about 107. The difference in the water temperature at which the eggs develop and hatch may well result in a greater number of vertebrae. Thus, perhaps, Europe gets its eel population from America.

However satisfying this hypothesis, it has not gained general acceptance. Some recent serological research carried out at Rutgers University strongly suggests a marked difference in these two populations.

In addition to the eel spawning area in the Sargasso Sea, there is another in the western North Pacific from which the Japanese eel larvae are carried by circulating currents to the Chinese coast as well as Japan. There is a third in the western South Pacific from which the Australian eel is carried to southeastern Australia, Tasmania and New Zealand, and a fourth in the Indian Ocean. There are no other eel spawning grounds known anywhere in the world and fresh-water eels occur only where coasts are washed by currents circulating from these three spawning areas. Thus there are no fresh-water eels in the western areas of the United States and Canada or in South America, and none in western Africa except on the north coast.

BUCKING THE CURRENTS OF A BRITISH COLUMBIA RIVER, SOCKEYE SALMON IN RED BREEDING LIVERY JOURNEY TO THEIR SPAWNING GROUNDS

The Far Travelers

Gorging in the plenty of the sea, how does the sleek salmon know when to start the long and arduous journey back to the stream of its birth? What guides it on the way? Why do the schools of fish appear in certain waters at certain times, as regularly as clockwork? What governs their shifting formations? We watch these wonders and strive to probe their meanings—but many mysteries remain.

CANADA

MT. BAKE

VANCOUVER

VICTORIA   MT. OLYMPUS

QUEEN CHARLOTTE ISLANDS   VANCOUVER ISLAND   CAPE FLATTERY

3RD AND 4TH YEAR SALMON
36 INCHES

2ND YEAR SALMON
18 TO 24 INCHES

"BLOOM" OF PLANKTON

←————— DAVIDSON CURRENT

SEA LION   DIVING DUCKS

SEALS   LOONS   GREBES

YOUNG SALMON HEADING NORTH

MATURE CHINOOK SALMON—
AVERAGE WEIGHT 24 LB.

The Ocean Odyssey
of the Chinook Salmon

The travels of fishes are as mysterious as their sometimes enormous aggregations. Some of the biggest
of them—the sharks, marlins, swordfish—are often
loners, shunning companionship. Others wander in
schools, like the anchovies and the tuna which feed
on them. But the Chinook salmon of the Pacific is a

COLUMBIA LAKE

GRAND COULEE

MT. RAINIER

COLUMBIA BASIN

MT. ST. HELENS

MT. ADAMS

SEATTLE

OLYMPIA

W A S H I N G T O N

GRAYS HARBOR

CHINOOK

COLUMBIA RIVER

ASTORIA

OREGON

1ST AND 2ND YEAR SALMON HEAD NORTH
UP TO 15 INCHES

PURSE SEINER

TROLLER

A FEW YOUNG SALMON GO SOUTH

MATURE CHINOOK IN 5TH YEAR
RETURN TO THEIR "MOTHER" RIVER

LING COD

SEA BASS

ASTORIA
CANYON

SEA LAMPREY

SOUP-FIN SHARK

DOGFISH SHARK

rolf klep

100 FATHOM LINE—EDGE OF CONTINENTAL SHELF

traveler with one purpose: getting back to spawn where it was born, after four years at sea. Drifting as a silvery smolt down from the upper reaches of the Columbia River, the Chinook starts its sea journey as a plankton feeder. As it grows, it turns predator, feeding on herring and other small fishes. Sharks and other large fishes, lampreys, sea lions, birds and men prey on it in turn. Running a four-year gantlet, the Chinook travels 700 miles to beyond the Queen Charlotte Islands before it turns back, gripped by the urge to spawn. How it finds its way to the very creek that gave it life is not known.

A FISHERMAN'S NET, whether wielded commercially or for research, is only one of many perils sockeyes face on the upstream run. The netted females will lose their eggs to a hatchery.

CLEARING UPSTREAM RAPIDS, a salmon negotiates white water in long leaps. At a high fall, salmon may jump eight feet or more, falling back repeatedly to try again until exhausted.

AN ENEMY FROM THE FOREST, this big brown bear seizes a thrashing chum salmon from the McNeil River in Alaska. In June and July, when the run is on, brown bears feed almost entirely on salmon, each staking out likely fishing territories and scooping up as many as 15 fish a day from the water while gulls and eagles, waiting for scraps, scream and wheel overhead.

Fight for Life on the Upstream Journey

Salmon face many dangers in their periods of growth and wandering out in the open sea, but paradoxically, their fiercest challenge—and their final one—comes when they return to make their way back up their home rivers. Here every foot forward is a battle against the current, with foaming rapids and roaring falls often barring the way. Sometimes man imposes even greater barriers—huge dams which the salmon can pass only with the help of elaborate fish ladders, elevators and side runs. Many of them never make it through the maze, and some of those that do may get lost in the currentless expanse of the reservoirs beyond. Those that make it to the smaller streams above face an army of predators. Fishermen take their harvest with net and rods and gaffs. Hungry bears wait for them, and birds of prey swoop down. Sometimes only a fraction of the throng that started upstream reaches its goal.

SPAWNING ACCOMPLISHED, dead and dying sockeyes drift downstream with the current, to collect in quiet eddies. After beating their way upstream, sometimes for hundreds of miles, the fish have used up all of their body fat. The struggle has left them bruised, battered, exhausted. The last of their energy is expended in spawning. This vital act finished, the salmon die.

Safety in Numbers

Like some 4,000 other species of fishes, salmon are schooling fish, and if their final desperate run upstream is accomplished more by individual strength and determination than by the massed strength of the school, this is primarily because the nature of the upstream hazards tends to put each fish on its own. It should not obscure the fact that fish schools have developed, through evolution, into basic protective devices which guarantee the survival of the greatest numbers under the many pressures of predation to which fish are subjected.

Simply by concentrating their numbers in schools, fish limit the areas in the sea in which they can be found and attacked. Then again, by massing their formations they present an aspect which may frighten smaller predators away, and also give each other a greater measure of protection against the larger fish which will attack them anyway. Perhaps because of this, most schools of smaller fishes tend to condense themselves, when actually threatened, into such tightly packed, milling balls of thousands of individuals as the bocaccio shown on the right.

A SCHOOLING THRONG of fish swims through coral formations near Florida's Key Largo. This huge aggregation, nearly 100 feet in diameter, is a characteristic protective association.

A MILLING BALL of bocaccio forms under the stern of a small boat. This unusual photograph, taken near Catalina Island, illustrates a type of fish formation which is rarely seen and which

A FORMATION OF TUNA knifes through the waters of the Gulf Stream, near the Bahamas. Sweeping northward, the fish may appear off Long Island in the summer, off Nova Scotia in the fall.

is usually the result of a school of fish being disturbed or alarmed. Each individual tries to hide behind its companions, and thus a ball is formed, exposing the least number to external danger.

A SWIRLING MASS of catfish swarms over sandy shallows in search of food. A tropical estuary dweller, this Indo-Pacific species has poison glands which empty through spines in its fins.

A VAST SCHOOL of thread herring, packed solidly in the sea, swims through clear Caribbean waters off the Virgin Islands. As members of the herring family—which includes sardines and several hundred other species—they belong to the most important group of food fishes in the world. Herring are easy prey for fishermen's nets because they school in astronomical numbers and in many cases appear almost as predictably as tides in certain places and at certain times to feed or spawn. A single school, several miles long and wide, may include billions of individual fish. The Bermuda chubs hovering over this close-packed throng do not prey on the herring, but may simply be following them out of curiosity, as they follow ships far out to sea.

8

The Costly Struggle to Harvest the Sea

I N 1883 Thomas Henry Huxley, one of the great scientific minds of his time, expressed an opinion that man has held about the sea for many centuries. "I believe," he said, at the Fisheries Exhibition in London, "probably all the great sea-fisheries are inexhaustible; that is to say, that nothing we do seriously affects the numbers of fish." Yet today, nearly a century later, Huxley's words, so bright with confidence at the time, have a ring of hollow irony, for man has at last begun to realize that the sea, for all of its seemingly infinite plenty, has its limits as a source of food.

Men have fished for as long as they have hunted, and that is a good long time. Always they have taken the resources of the waters for granted, and as populations grew and nations industrialized, they have expanded and industrialized their fisheries to keep pace with the increased demand. For fish is one of the staple foods, one of the richest of all sources of animal protein, and in a world faced with a population explosion it may be essential to mankind's continued survival. The amount of fish taken from the world's waters has been rising year by year and today it totals about 64 million metric tons. Some 30 per cent of this total is consumed fresh while the rest is cured, canned, frozen, rendered into fish meal or processed into fertilizer. And about 85 per cent of the total comes from the sea.

Yet fish and seafood still account for only a small fraction of the world's total supply of protein. Thus the outlook for the future is one of even greater increases in the harvesting of fish—and this at a time when man has only just begun to try safeguarding the supply of food fish and if possible increasing it.

Five countries contribute half of the world's total harvest of sea and fresh-water fish. Japan was long the leading fishing nation, but her recent catches —in excess of eight million metric tons a year—are now surpassed by those of Peru; with the swarms of anchoveta just off her coast, this nation takes in more than 10 million metric tons of fish annually. Although no recent estimates are available, Communist China probably belongs to the top three, with much of the catch coming from fresh-water ponds. Soviet Russia is ranked fourth, with an annual catch of more than six million metric tons. The United States is fifth, having replaced Norway, whose herring stocks have dwindled drastically. India, Spain, Denmark, Canada, Chile, Thailand and the United Kingdom are next on the list, each catching more than a million metric tons a year.

BY far the largest portion of the world's fisheries, in both the temperate and tropical zones, lies in the offshore waters of the continents in depths of less than 200 fathoms. All these continental shelves combined occupy only about 10 per cent of the area of the oceans, but the amount of fish they produce is disproportionately huge. For these are the regions where conditions are most suitable for an abundance of sea life. Here the plankton thrives, as do the many plants and creatures of the bottom, providing the food for a vast population of bottom-dwelling and pelagic fishes. Here are the great harvest grounds, by comparison to which the open ocean with its far-flung wanderers, such as the tuna and the albacore, is a commercial wasteland. And here, just offshore, the fishing nations of the world are engaged in a competitive struggle to reap the riches of the sea which is as unrelenting as it is fraught with ultimate peril for the food-fish population as a whole.

The tools employed to harvest the sea are of many diverse types, and in recent

COMMERCIAL FISHING AREAS

The major fishing areas of the world lie along the sloping shelves of the continents. The most extensively exploited of these regions are in dark blue on the map. Bordering them are less exploited areas, shown in medium blue, which are also rich in aquatic life and have possibilities for expansion. Areas where there has been little or no exploitation but where the resources are good are indicated in pale blue.

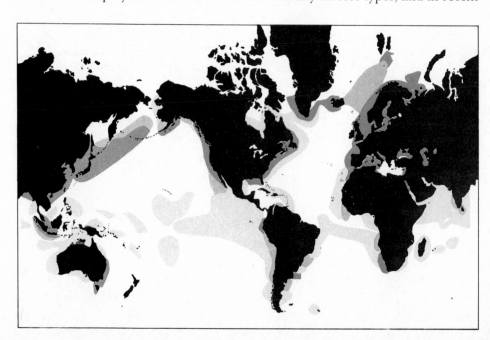

years their efficiency has increased to a degree that is cause for serious concern. Whereas 50 years ago the fishing fleets of most of the world's nations consisted mainly of single vessels going out with trawls, purse seines and dories laying long lines, today they are composed of entire flotillas complete with mother ships, spotters, catchers and floating factories to process immediately the fish caught. And while the otter trawl, the great, wide-mouthed net towed along the sea bottom or in the middle depths, and the purse seine remain the basic catching tools, they are used with far greater efficiency than ever before, and in conjunction with a wide variety of fishing aids. Planes are sent out to find schools of fish, and echo sounders can even locate fish lying on the bottom. In the offing are television cameras towed under water to provide visual clues for the fishermen above, and fishing vessels which will be almost automatic—electronic computers coupled to the television cameras will steer the trawls and adjust their depths to intercept the fish at their own level.

Meanwhile, aboard ocean-traveling research vessels and in laboratories on land, scientists are working at ever more ingenious ways of finding, catching and processing fish. Oceanography is now recognized as one of the most important fields of study in relation to the burning question of the world's food supply. Fisheries biology, involving as it does research into such vital matters as the growth of fishes, their feeding habits, the mechanism governing their schooling and migrations and many other factors directly applicable to their living and dying, is receiving the support of governments where not long ago it was dependent on the interest of private philanthropy. The big question is: can man learn to perfect techniques for sowing the sea as well as for reaping it? The answer to this question is fateful to much of the world's population, particularly in new and underdeveloped nations. Today one half of the people on this planet are chronically undernourished. Aside from increased crops brought by the "green revolution," their best hope of augmenting their available food supplies lies in the sea.

How serious is the actual threat to the world's fish supply? We know that the trawlers of many nations have been compelled to go farther and farther afield for larger catches. The Japanese now fish in every ocean; Russian trawlers by the score fish the banks between Cape Cod and Nova Scotia and, on the other side of North America, are pushing ever deeper into the oceans of the world. With all of these widespread activities, the statistics on the total catch seem reassuring. But the statistics, as so often, are misleading.

The actual amount of fish landed in a given period is an unreliable guide to what is happening to a fishery. These figures over a period of a decade might reflect a steady rise, giving an impression of continuing abundance, whereas what they actually reflect is increasing fishing intensity—more boats, better equipment, all adding up to increasing pressure on the fish population. The total catch, or, as fisheries people call it, "total yield," of a fishery is the product of this fishing intensity and the catch per unit of effort—per boat or per man— and it is this latter that gives a realistic measure of the relative abundance of fish. As long as the catch per unit of effort does not drop, regardless of how many boats have been added to the fishing fleet, all is well—but when more and more effort is needed to increase or maintain the total yield, it is the first indication of a decline in abundance of the particular fish species concerned.

The eastern Pacific yellowfin-tuna fishery is a case in point. In the late 1930s and early 1940s the fishing intensity averaged about 8,000 standard days with a catch per standard day of about 9,000 pounds (a standard day is a unit of measurement calculated on the basis of the boats in a fleet and the days they can fish, to give fishery commissions a working rule to go by in setting catch limits). By the late 1950s, however, the fishing intensity averaged about 30,000 standard days—an almost fourfold increase—while the catch per day averaged about 5,000 pounds, a decline of close to one half. At the same time, the total yield averaged about 190 million pounds as against an average of 125 million pounds some 20 years ago.

Such an increase in the total yield might easily give the impression that the yellowfin-tuna fishery was thriving—actually, it has recently come to the verge of being overfished. It has been calculated that if the fishing intensity exceeds 35,000 standard days the fish population will be exploited faster than it can restore itself. Thus, in recent years, the Inter-American Tropical Tuna Commission has had to impose specific limits to avoid a decline in annual average catch of the yellowfin tuna in this part of the Pacific Ocean. For when a fish population is exploited faster than it naturally reproduces itself, a fatal spiral sets in and within a few years the fishery may fail.

One such decline in the Pacific halibut fishery in the 1920s led to the creation of an international fisheries commission, set up by the United States and Canadian governments, to study the question and make recommendations. More recently, there have been similar declines in the northwest Atlantic redfish, cod and haddock fisheries, and in the sardine fishery off the coast of California. Whether they are due chiefly or only in part to the predations of man is not clear. But one thing did become painfully clear: the number of small fish caught increased steadily, and the number of larger adult fish decreased. When that happens the population as a whole may be in danger.

EVALUATING changes of this kind on the fishing grounds is the job of the fishery research biologist. A man of increasing responsibility in the food picture of his country and the world, he faces a task that is often difficult and sometimes seemingly impossible, particularly where oceanic populations are concerned. Whereas his counterpart on land is able to follow the complete life cycle of an animal or animals under study from birth to death, taking precise note of every stage of its development, determining accurate population counts by actual observation, the fishery biologist is, as one man put it, "like a blindfolded man trying to find out what is happening at the bottom of a well." His fundamental problem is that he is dealing with something he cannot empirically measure with his own eyes. He may cast his nets and draw up samples of the fish popula-

THE DRIFT NET

This is used principally to catch herring and mackerel. A boat moves into a likely area before nightfall and "shoots" as much as three miles of net across the incoming or outgoing tide. With one end anchored to the vessel, the net hangs like a wall from the surface of the water, buoyed up by floats and weighted along the bottom with lead. Both boat and net drift throughout the night. When schooling fish try to pass through the net, their gill covers become tangled in the mesh, trapping them. Around dawn, the net is hauled in.

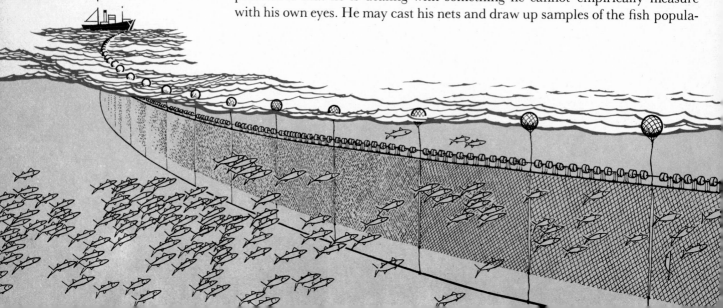

tion from the depths, but he cannot tell with any degree of certainty if his samples reflect the actual community down below. He cannot operate with any known, fixed values; all his figures can be arrived at only deductively. He can work only by building a model in his mind on the basis of what he thinks he knows, and then, in tedious, endlessly repeated research efforts and experiments, compare his findings to that model, changing it, rearranging it until at last it seems to fit. And even then he does not know, but only can surmise.

One of the most important tools in this enormous research effort is the fisheries research vessel, a floating laboratory equipped not only with modern devices for locating, tracking and catching fish at any depth, but also with an array of instruments for measuring salinity and chemical content of the waters, temperature, currents, composition of the bottom, study of organisms and microorganisms in the plankton and many other scientific matters, as well as a staff of scientists who make voyages of weeks and months at a time to probe these most important secrets of the sea. In addition, the fishery biologist has at his disposal such shore-based research centers as the U.S. Bureau of Commercial Fisheries Biological Laboratory at Woods Hole, Massachusetts, the Oceanographic Institution at the same location, the Scripps Institution of Oceanography at La Jolla, California, the Lerner Marine Laboratory at Bimini in the Bahamas, and many more throughout the world.

BIG as it is, the job of fishery research has inevitably grown beyond national boundaries and is being conducted more and more on an international basis under the aegis of international commissions, treaty conventions and through the United Nations. Only through cooperation on these levels can the problems of manpower and logistics involved in research on the many far-ranging marine species be adequately solved. And as sharp as the competition may be among the fishing fleets on the high seas, the realization that a common resource affecting the entire world is at stake is equally strong.

Thus international fishery treaty conventions are among the most successful and altruistic of all efforts at international cooperation in any field. Some have existed for a long time. Around the turn of the century the King of Sweden, Oscar II, instigated the formation of the International Council for the Exploration of the Sea. With its headquarters in the castle of Charlottenlund in Copenhagen, its task was to carry out scientific research into the stocks of fish in European waters and to make recommendations for the control of the fishing industries of its 16 member-nations. The council has survived two world wars and is still active and efficient today.

In Europe, with its language barriers and close national rivalries, such co-operation was less easily arrived at than in North America, where Canada and the United States benefit from both a common language and, to a great extent, common interests and traditions. Yet today, a dozen European countries share with North American nations membership in the International Commission for Northwest Atlantic Fisheries, the chief governing body enforcing fishery regulations and coordinating the marine biological research on the western side of the North Atlantic. Historically and economically, the interests of many nations converge on the waters between Cape Cod and Labrador. Spain, Portugal, Great Britain and France have been fishing there since the early 16th Century, and France's fishery interests are still represented by her two territorial possessions, the islands of St. Pierre and Miquelon.

THE PURSE SEINE

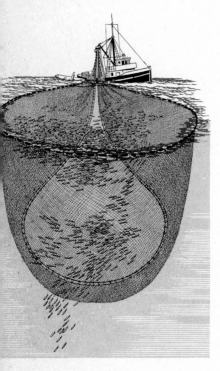

This net depends on the same principle as the drawstring of an old-fashioned purse. The boat circles a large school of fish, like tuna or menhaden, paying out the net as it goes along. A small seine boat, carrying the other end of the net, assists in the operation. When the school is completely encircled, a power block hooked up to the mast of the big boat pulls the bottom of the net together so that the fish cannot escape. A dip net then removes large fish; small ones are pumped up through a hose.

SINCE man cannot, as yet, sow the sea that he may reap by putting fish back into it, the problem of overfishing in the oceans necessarily must be dealt with by controlling fishing activities. And since all measures of control must turn on the evident fact that too many small, immature fish are swept up by the trawls, some feasible way of regulating the size of the individual fish caught becomes a matter of primary concern.

One way to do this is to close certain areas of the sea to fishing at those times of year when the young fish are known to be congregating there, just as many fresh-water lakes and rivers are closed to sportsmen in some seasons. This is one of the primary motives behind the effort of various nations to extend their territorial limits and thus assume authority to impose fishing limits in their off-shore waters. However, creating prohibited areas in the sea has obvious built-in difficulties and while, under certain circumstances, it is possible to fix a size limit and forbid the catching, landing or sale of any fish below that size, as a general solution to the problem it is far from being satisfactory in practice.

Another method is to regulate the size of the mesh in the nets used to catch fish. In the northwest Atlantic there have been mesh regulations in the cod and haddock fisheries for many years now. The principle is simple: in any net with meshes of a given size, some fish will be caught while smaller fish will slip through and escape. By regulating the size of the mesh so that fish above a certain size will be caught, the survival of the immature fish is, in theory, assured.

Mesh regulation is now an important part of fishery control, but it still has its imperfections. One derives from the fact that different fish of different species vary in size—a mature whiting, for example, is about the same size as an immature cod, so that a net designed to allow young cod to escape will also permit mature and perfectly salable whiting to get away. A great deal of experimentation is necessary before equitable mesh sizes can be arrived at. In most cases they are coupled with further regulations governing the size of the various species of fish that can be sold.

A third method of controlling the fisheries is to create more of them—by devices such as transplanting fish themselves into areas where they might thrive. As farfetched as this may seem, considering the vast reaches of the sea, several such experiments have been attempted, so far with only limited success. The eggs of the shad, collected and hatched on the Atlantic coast of the United States, were successfully transferred to the mouth of the Sacramento River in California and have created an artificial shad fishery there. Striped bass, as mentioned earlier, were transplanted in the same way to waters around San Francisco. Recently Soviet Russia has attempted to transfer Pacific salmon as very young fish to northern European waters; the results seem promising and some of the salmon have appeared as adults in Scottish rivers and on Norwegian spawning grounds. Similarly, herring have been transplanted from the Baltic to the Aral Sea. But none of these experiments, with the exception of the shad transfer, could be done on a large enough scale to affect the fisheries to any commercially important extent. The sea is simply too big, its population of fishes too huge, its currents, temperatures, chemical content too uncontrollable for man's efforts to be more than the proverbial drop in the bucket. When one considers that just one relatively small, if important, fishing area, the Georges Banks off Cape Cod, covers 10,000 square miles and harbors perhaps billions of fishes, the magnitude of the effort required to influence its ecology to any meaningful degree is obvious.

The sea remains, in all its vastness, a constantly tantalizing challenge to the human community which sees itself running short of food. At an International Conference on Fish in Nutrition, held in Washington under the sponsorship of the United Nations Food and Agriculture Organization, it was clearly brought out that in large parts of the world, especially where there is a high potential for development, the first requisite for improving living conditions was to increase the supply of protein foodstuffs, which is tantamount to increasing the harvest of fish. What can be done?

Since the dangers of overfishing have already been referred to, it may seem paradoxical to suggest that one way would be to increase the efficiency of some of the fishermen in the world. Actually, this is a way. While some of the great, traditional fishing grounds are in danger of being overfished, other areas, notably in territorial waters around some of the less advanced nations, could support far heavier commercial fishing. Often, this is a matter of simple know-how and equipment, as a recent example from Ecuador shows.

There are more than 100 small fishing villages along the coast of Ecuador which are home ports for some 10,000 fishermen. And although there are some modern plants for processing and exporting shrimp and tuna, the fishing itself is done with methods and equipment dating back hundreds of years. Three main types of boat are used—balsa rafts rigged with sails; dugout canoes hewn from cedar logs; and planked sailboats up to 35 feet in length. Nets are for the most part handmade from cotton fibers; the durable nylon netting now used in virtually all modern fisheries is prohibitively expensive in this area.

To these coastal villages in February 1958 the United Nations Food and Agriculture Organization sent a young American master fisherman named Erling Oswald, who brought with him one small diesel engine and an assortment of nylon nets and lines, fishing lures, mechanical and hand winches and fishing lamps, all provided by the FAO. The Ecuadorian government supplied Oswald with a 23-foot sailboat. He installed the engine, hired a crew and went to work.

The result, to the Ecuadorians, was startling. With his one small, engine-driven boat and modern equipment, Oswald delivered more than half a ton of tuna daily, almost as much as the total daily catch made by all the unmechanized canoes and sailboats used by the fishermen of the town of Manta, where he began his demonstrations. Oswald also demonstrated the greatly improved fishing techniques made possible by modern equipment. But even more important, he demonstrated that this equipment, once put to use, quickly paid for itself. In two years, during which time all of the costs of the boat he used were paid for by the fish he caught, he started a small revolution among these Ecua-

THE TRAWL NET

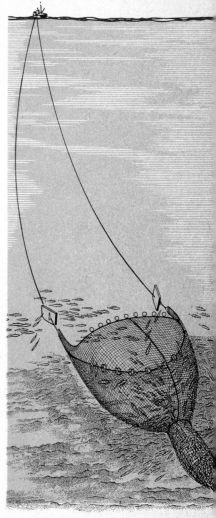

One of the commonest of all commercial nets, the otter trawl harvests bottom-dwelling fish like cod and plaice. As it sweeps along the bottom, two very heavy, ironbound wood "otter doors" are used to keep the nets open, while a footrope along its lower lip roils the sand and frightens the fish into the cod end at the rear of the net. After the net has been down long enough for a good catch (sometimes at depths of 400 to 500 fathoms), it is hauled aboard with a strong winch.

dorian fishermen who for so long had been unable to improve on the old ways.

The revolution bore fruit when, with the help of the U.S. International Cooperation Administration and the Ecuadorian Ministry of Social Welfare, $6,000 was provided for the purchase of several small diesel engines. Denmark sent a marine engineer to help install them and to train the fishermen in their operation and maintenance. The fishermen, in turn, modified their boats at their own expense. The FAO loaned them nylon gill nets. Thus equipped, one 25-foot boat from Santa Rosa brought in almost 34,000 pounds of pompano, spadefish, sierra and tuna in its first 14 days of operations—this despite the fact that the best part of the fishing season was over for that year. The original credit of $6,000 was shortly paid off, and additional funds of $10,000, six more diesel engines and more than 2,000 pounds of nylon webbing and twine were secured. So encouraging were the results that the Ecuadorian government itself embarked on a four-year, $633,000 program to broaden Oswald's work. The days of the balsa raft and the dugout canoe along Ecuador's coast, as the result of one man's work, are already numbered.

ECUADOR is an example of how, in some areas of the world, fishing efficiency can be increased and more fish taken without any danger of overfishing the existing population. The same techniques could be very profitably applied in many parts of Africa, Asia and the Far East. The FAO, studying this matter, has suggested that the Arabian Sea, the Persian Gulf, the southern waters of Australia and the west coast of South America in general are all capable of supporting profitable fishing industries. As an example, South Africa in recent years has developed a thriving pilchard fishery, and similar successes have been reported by India, Ceylon and other Far East countries.

In startling contrast to such expanding activities is the extraordinary decline of one of the great fishing powers of the world—the United States. Because of the stubbornly antiquated methods of a large proportion of American fishermen, the high cost of building new equipment in this country and an incredible 1792 law still on the books which forbids American fishermen to land catches in any but American-built boats, this country's share of the world fishery production is down to less than 4 per cent, from 13 per cent in 1948. Fishery research in the United States is qualitatively on a par with the best in the world, but in its resources it lags considerably behind such leading competitive nations as the Soviet Union and Japan. Much of the technological equipment of the United States fishing fleet is virtually obsolete. Whereas the other leading fishing nations send out fleets equipped to process fish on the high seas, many American fishermen must still bring their catch back to port before it can be handled. And in the combined fleets of the once-great ports of Boston and Gloucester, 500 strong at the end of World War II, the largest vessel is smaller than the smallest boat in the Soviet fleet of more than 200 modern craft which in recent years has been in almost constant operation off Cape Cod.

Along with modern fishing methods and control, another important factor in increasing the world supply of protein foods through fish is to utilize more effectively the fish caught. One of the most promising ways of doing this lies in the manufacture of fish meal and flour, which not only make full use of all parts of the commercial food fish but also of what fishermen call trash fish—skates, dogfish, searobins and others that often make up half the catch of a trawler and are ordinarily thrown away.

Norway began research on fish meal for human consumption as far back as the late 1880s, and since then a great deal has been done. Germany, on strict rations in World War II, used fish meal as an egg substitute. Peru today produces some 1,900,000 tons annually. Fish protein concentrate (FPC), a recent development in the United States, is derived by converting the entire fish, scales, viscera and all, into a colorless, odorless, chemically pure white powder that is rich in animal proteins and can be used in a variety of ways—in stews, vegetable dishes, or mixed with wheat flour. FPC has already proved a remarkably efficient curative for protein-deficiency diseases. Best of all, it is so cheap to manufacture that the entire animal protein needs of the world's population could be met with FPC at a cost of only half a cent per person a day.

Yet the question still remains—will the world supply of fish be able to resist indefinitely the steady increase in the world's fishing power? Will we ever be able to replenish and even greatly increase that supply by effectively cultivating fish in our waters as farmers cultivate their crops on land?

In fresh water, fish cultivation is an old story—and one which can profitably be brought up to date. Fish have been raised for centuries in ponds and rice paddies in the Orient; in Europe carp have been cultivated since the Middle Ages, when every monastery and many a feudal lord's castle had its carp pond. Even today, mainland China gets almost half of its annual catch from inland fresh-water sources. In the lower Mississippi states, a thriving industry of catfish culture has grown up. And yet, the potentialities of fresh-water-fish cultivation have barely begun to be exploited. With the knowledge gained by modern research, it has become quite clear that the production of fresh-water fishes could be enormously increased.

THUS, for example, the FAO estimates that there are 91,427,000 acres of cultivable inland waters in the Indo-Pacific region alone. There are additional fresh-water resources in Africa and Central America where fish could not only be made available through cultivation, but made available right where they are most needed, in protein-starved, underdeveloped countries. Furthermore, fish cultivation in rice paddies, as in the Far East, has been shown to have a beneficial effect on the rice crop since the fish feed on insect, plant and animal pests—this, obviously, is of additional importance to the over-all food picture in such areas.

Fresh-water fishes do lend themselves to cultivation, and represent a hope for the future in the world's food supply. But how, apart from such relatively puny efforts as the fish transplantings mentioned earlier, can man ever cultivate the vastness of the sea?

Some promising beginnings—and some startling proposals—have been made. Shortly after World War II experiments were carried out to speed up fish growth in several lochs of Scotland. Partially open to the sea, these lochs were manured with chemicals in the spring and early summer. The immediate result was an immense increase in the animal and plant plankton. Plaice were then introduced into the lochs to thrive on the rich food supply. Not only did they thrive, they added two years' growth in six months' time and matured correspondingly early, a direct result of a similar growth increase in the mollusks and other creatures of the bottom on which they fed.

Here, then, was a possibility of artificially speeding up the growth of fishes by fertilizing the plankton and other foodstuff on which fishes feed, much as hay, alfalfa and other grazing crops are fertilized on land. But is this feasible in the open sea, even in the waters close to shore?

Sir Alister Hardy, professor of zoology at Oxford and a world-famous marine biologist, has suggested that small areas of the sea might be fertilized by towing the organic waste of cities out to sea in lighters, dumping it where there are no strong currents to disperse it. Going even further, he has proposed that the bottom of the sea itself, where so many food fishes feed, might be plowed and harrowed to eliminate such pests as starfishes which compete with the fishes for food. "I have imagined," writes Hardy, "the fishermen of a hundred years hence being frogmen working tractor-driven trawls sent down from a parent ship above, and then at intervals teams of sub-aqua-men whirring backwards and forwards over the sea bed driving the latest patterns of starfish eradicators." French undersea explorer Jacques-Yves Cousteau plans to build an entire underwater village of prefabricated houses in which 24 men could live for several weeks. The first such house was tested in the summer of 1963, when seven of Cousteau's crew spent a month in it, five fathoms under the Red Sea. He also conjectures—nonbiologically, of course—the evolution of a new species, *Homo aquaticus*, equipped with an artificial gill containing chemicals which would allow the user to regenerate his blood oxygen from sea water.

Perhaps more immediately realistic are proposals to culture fish fry in huge tanks where they would feed on plankton which itself would be cultured in bulk. Once these artificially reared fish had passed the critical stage in their development, they would then be set free in the sea. Although the experiments in the lochs of Scotland point the way to such projects, the main question still is: can even relatively large efforts along these lines have any real effect on the tremendous populations of the sea?

So far, despite all the efforts, all the research, all the plans, man's best hope seems to lie in exercising reasonable control over the heavily exploited fisheries of the continental shelves and at the same time seeking new areas whose fish resources can still be harvested without endangering the fish population. Yet now is the time to take warning. In the whaling industry the fishing power has increased to the point where the population of whales is so reduced and the expeditions themselves are so expensive to equip and send out that few are still profitable. Several types of whales are now on the "endangered species" list. How long will it be before that point is reached in other fisheries?

In the North Atlantic, the most heavily fished area of the world, it already has been reached. The herring population is decreasing and haddock has been virtually wiped out. In the tropical areas, whose countries swarm with a fish-hungry population but are poor in technical know-how and in the ancient, tough traditions of skill and hard work at sea, it may be a long way off still.

Certain it is that the control of fishing activities and the possibility of adding more fish to the sea as the stocks are depleted cannot come about without a detailed knowledge of the natural history of fishes, their feeding and breeding habits, their growth, their migrations and all aspects of the watery world in which they live. For the better part of half a century all the great nations of the world have had their own organizations for carrying out this kind of fishery research in their own waters and in the waters exploited by their fishermen. More recently, they have to an increasing degree pooled their investigative resources and the knowledge gained in international organizations working on these worldwide problems for the good of all. These international programs, in addition to helping to resolve the urgent task of feeding the world's hungry peoples, may well be setting the stage for the broader cooperation and understanding among nations which is the paramount necessity facing mankind today.

A FISHERMAN ON THE BLACK VOLTA IN AFRICA CASTS HIS WEIGHTED NET INTO THE WATER FOR A CATCH OF BOLTI, BICHIR OR CATFISH

Fish as Food

With more than half the world's population in need of protein, men everywhere are seeking more efficient ways of harvesting one of the richest, most abundant sources available—fish. Already many of the technologically advanced nations have modernized their fishing fleets. But as the world's catch goes up, steps must be taken to prevent some areas from being overfished by competing nations.

SEVENTY PORTUGUESE FISHERMEN struggle to launch a sardine boat in the booming surf. These boats are very heavy and they lie on the beach, the shallow water of the receding waves swirling around them. The men with the ropes steady the boat and keep it pointing seaward so that it will not be swung broadside by an incoming wave and swamped. When a wave does

come in, enough water surges under the keel for the men at the oars, pulling mightily, to get it out into deeper water. Once beyond the surf the crew will use a large net to scoop up the sardines which swarm in the warm Portuguese waters. Sardines constitute 40 per cent of Portugal's annual catch, which in 1961 amounted to 134,474 metric tons and was valued at $14 million.

The Battle on the Banks

Proud old dory-schooners like the Portuguese vessel below were a familiar sight through generations of fishermen on the Grand Banks of Newfoundland, the greatest single cod fishery in the world. Here, on "the silver mines of the sea," as many as 15 nations, including the Soviet Union, East Germany, Poland and lately even Japan, are still in fierce competition. But the fine old schooners are fast disappearing as fleets of fishing vessels complete with floating factories move in. Radar, echo sounders and airplane spotters combine to increase the heavy pressure on the fishes. Yet in the face of all this foreign rivalry,

WITH DAWN'S ARRIVAL ON THE GRAND BANKS, PORTUGUESE FISHERMEN SET OUT IN TINY ONE-MAN DORIES FOR A LONELY DAY'S FISHING. THEY

the United States, now in sixth place among the leading fishing nations of the world, is losing ground as steadily as the fishes themselves, hampered by high costs, an ancient law forbidding fishermen to buy new boats abroad, and a stubborn Yankee adherence to outmoded fishing techniques.

U.S. DRAGGERS, docked at Gloucester, are losing out in a competition with other countries that use bigger fishing boats.

USE HAND LINES, STRUNG WITH 400 TO 1,000 HOOKS, AN OLD METHOD, FAST DYING OUT, THAT BRINGS IN FEWER BUT BIGGER COD THAN NETS

IN A NORWEGIAN VILLAGE, COD HANG TO DRY BY THE THOUSANDS, BUT THE BOATS BEYOND MUST WORK HARD TO KEEP UP THE SUPPLY

Overfishing—and the Answer

The dangers of overfishing on the Grand Banks are still only a threat, but across the Atlantic on the great cod grounds of Norway's Lofoten Islands, they are very real. For centuries cod have returned to the Lofotens in the tens of millions to spawn, but recently the runs have thinned. Some experts argue that the giant trawlers of the Soviet Union and other countries are sweeping up immature fish in the Barents Sea before they can return home to spawn. Those that do get back find a hard-pressed Norwegian fishing fleet waiting for them. One way to protect these grounds lies in international agreements controlling catches. How effective this can be is shown by the dramatic story of the Pacific sockeye salmon. This species was restored to abundance by a U.S.-Canadian treaty allowing it to swim unmolested to its spawning grounds during regulated periods—thus assuring its renewal in the millions.

IN A CANADIAN PLANT, ceiling-high stacks of frozen salmon, part of a $41 million catch, tell of the success the U.S. and Canada have had in restoring sockeye to Canada's Fraser River.

Appendix

Common and Scientific Names of Fishes

Albacore *Thunnus alalunga*
Alewife *Alosa pseudoharengus*
Anchoveta *Cetengraulis mysticetus*
Anchovy, European *Engraulis encrasicholus*
Anchovy, Pacific or Northern *Engraulis mordax*
Angelfish, Fresh-water *Pterophyllum eimekei*
Angelfish, Queen *Holacanthus ciliaris*
Angler, Deep-sea *Borophryne apogon*
Angler, Yellow *Antennarius moluccensis*
Archerfish *Toxotes jaculatrix*
Barracuda, Great *Sphyraena barracuda*
Barracuda, Pacific *Sphyraena argentea*
Bass, Black Sea *Centropristes striatus*
Bass, Calico *Pomoxis nigromaculatus*
Bass, Largemouth *Micropterus salmoides*
Bass, Smallmouth *Micropterus dolomieu*
Batfish, Torpedo *Halieutaea retifera*
Bichir *Polypterus bichir*
Bitterling *Rhodeus sericeus*
Blenny, Saber-toothed *Aspidontus rhinorhynchus*
Bluefish *Pomatomus saltatrix*
Bluegill *Lepomis macrochirus*
Bocaccio (Pacific Rockfish) *Sebastodes paucispinis*
Bolti *Tilapia nilotica*
Bonito, Atlantic *Sarda sarda*
Bonito, Pacific *Sarda chiliensis*
Bowfin *Amia calva*
Bullhead, Black *Ictalurus melas*
Bullhead, Brown *Ictalurus nebulosus*
Bullhead, Yellow *Ictalurus natalis*
Burbot *Lota lota*
Butterflyfish *Heniochus nigrirostris*
Candiru *Hemicetopsis candira, Vandellia cirrhosa*
Capelin, Atlantic *Mallotus villosus*
Carp *Cyprinus carpio*
Catfish, Glass *Kryptopterus bicirrhis*
Characin *Copeina arnoldi*
Chub, Bermuda *Kyphosus sectatrix*
Clingfish *Lepadogaster candolli*
Cod, Atlantic *Gadus morhua*
Coelacanth *Latimeria chalumnae*
Crappie, Black *Pomoxis nigromaculatus*
Crappie, White *Pomoxis annularis*
Dace, Black-nosed *Rhinichthys atratulus*
Darter, Shield *Percina peltata*
Discus Fish *Symphysodon discus*
Dogfish, Smooth (of eastern Pacific) *Mustelus californicus*
Dogfish, Spiny *Squalus acanthias*
Dolphin (Dorado) *Coryphaena hippurus*
Dragonet, Coral *Callionymus boekei*
Dragonet, European *Callionymus lyra*
Drum, Fresh-water *Aplodinotus grunniens*
Eel, American *Anguilla rostrata*
Eel, European *Anguilla anguilla*
Eel, Dragon Moray *Mureana pardalis*
Eel, Green Moray *Gymnothorax funebris*
Eel, Moray *Gymnothorax eurostus*
Flounder, Summer *Paralichthys dentatus*
Flounder, Winter *Pseudopleuronectes americanus*
Flyingfish, California *Cypselurus californicus*
Gar, Alligator *Lepisosteus spatula*
Goby, Dwarf Pygmy *Pandaka pygmaea*
Goby, Highfin *Gobionellus oceanicus*
Goldfish *Carassius auratus*
Goosefish *Lophius americanus*
Gourami, Giant *Osphronemus goramy*
Grouper, Nassau *Epinephelus striatus*
Grouper, Red *Epinephelus morio*
Grunion, California *Leuresthes tenuis*
Grunt, French *Haemulon flavolineatum*

Guitarfish, Spotted *Rhinobatos lentiginosus*
Guppy *Lebistes reticulatus*
Gurnard, Flying *Dactylopterus volitans*
Haddock *Melanogrammus aeglefinus*
Hake, European *Merluccius merluccius*
Hake, Silver *Merluccius bilinearis*
Hake, Southern *Urophycis floridanus*
Halibut, Atlantic *Hippoglossus hippoglossus*
Herring, Atlantic *Clupea harengus harengus*
Herring, Cisco or Lake *Coregonus artedi*
Herring, Thread *Opisthonema oglinum*
Jack, Crevallé *Caranx hippos*
Jack, Yellow *Caranx bartholomaei*
Jawfish, Yellow-headed *Opisthognathus aurifrons*
Jewfish, Spotted *Promicrops itaiara*
Lamprey, Brook *Entosphenus lamottenii*
Lamprey, Sea *Petromyzon marinus*
Lancet Fish, Pacific *Alepisaurus richardsoni*
Launce, American Sand *Ammodytes americanus*
Leaf Fish, Amazon *Monocirrhus polyacanthus*
Lingcod *Ophiodon elongatus*
Lionfish (Zebra Fish) *Pterois volitans*
Lungfish, Australian *Neoceratodus forsteri*
Mackerel, King *Scomberomorus cavalla*
Mackerel, Pacific *Scomber japonicus*
Mahseer *Barbus tor*
Man-of-War Fish *Nomeus gronovii*
Marlin, Black *Istiompax indicus*
Marlin, Blue *Makaira nigricans*
Menhaden, Atlantic *Brevoortia tyrannus*
Molly, Amazon *Mollienisia formosa*
Molly, Sailfin *Mollienisia latipinna*
Mormyrid, Ubangi *Gnathonemus petersi*
Mouthbreeder, West African *Tilapia macrocephala*
Mudskipper *Periophthalmus koelreuteri*
Mullet, Red (Surmullet) *Mullus surmuletus*
Mummichog *Fundulus heteroclitus*
Paddlefish *Polyodon spathula*
Parrotfish, Blue *Scarus coeruleus*
Pearlfish *Carapus bermudensis*
Perch, Climbing *Anabas testudineus*
Perch, Yellow *Perca flavescens*
Pickerel, Chain (Pike) *Esox niger*
Pike, Northern *Esox lucius*
Pilotfish *Naucrates ductor*
Pipefish, Banded *Dunckerocampus caullervi chapmani*
Pipefish, Bay *Syngnathus griseolineatus*
Piranha *Serrasalmus nattereri*
Plaice, American *Hippoglossoides platessoides*
Pollack *Pollachius virens*
Pompano, African *Alectis crinitus*
Porcupinefish *Diodon holocanthus*
Porgy, Silver *Diplodus argenteus*
Porkfish *Anisotremus virginicus*
Pout, Ocean *Macrozoarces americanus*
Pumpkinseed *Lepomis gibbosus*
Ratfish *Hydrolagus colliei*
Ray, Cow-nosed *Rhinoptera bonasus*
Ray, Manta (Devilfish) *Manta birostris*
Redfish *Sebastes marinus*
Redfish, Giant *Arapaima gigas*
Salmon, Chum *Oncorhynchus keta*
Salmon, King or Chinook *Oncorhynchus tshawytscha*
Salmon, Pink *Oncorhynchus gorbuscha*
Salmon, Sockeye *Oncorhynchus nerka*
Sardine, California *Sardinops sagax*
Sardine (Pilchard) *Sardina pilchardus*
Sargassum Fish (Frogfish) *Histrio histrio*
Sawfish *Pristis pectinatus*

Scorpion Fish *Scorpaena gibbosa*
Scup, Northern (Porgy) *Stenotomus chrysops*
Seahorse, Atlantic *Hippocampus hudsonius*
Seaperch, Black *Embiotica jacksoni*
Searobin, Common *Prionotus carolinus*
Shad, American *Alosa sapidissima*
Shark, Angel *Squatina dumerili*
Shark, Basking *Cetorhinus maximus*
Shark, Black-tipped *Carcharhinus melanopterus*
Shark, Blue *Prionace glauca*
Shark, Common Nurse *Ginglyostoma cirratum*
Shark, Grey Nurse *Carcharias arenarius*
Shark, Hammerhead *Sphyrna diplana*
Shark, Lemon *Negaprion brevirostris*
Shark, Leopard *Triakis semifasciata*
Shark, Mako *Isurus oxyrinchus*
Shark, Port Jackson *Heterodontus philippi*
Shark, Sand *Carcharias taurus*
Shark, Smooth Hammerhead *Sphyrna zygaena*
Shark, Thresher *Alopias vulpinus*
Shark, Tiger *Galeocerdo cuvier*
Shark, Whale *Rhincodon typus*
Shark, White *Carcharodon carcharias*
Shark Sucker (Remora) *Echeneis naucrates*
Shiner, Golden *Notemigonus crysoleucas*
Siamese Fighting Fish (Betta) *Betta splendens*
Silver Jenny *Eucinostomus gula*
Skate, Big *Raja binoculata*
Skate, Little *Raja erinacea*
Skate, Texas *Raja texana*
Skate, Thornback *Raja clavata*
Smelt, American *Osmerus mordax*
Smelt, Surf *Hypomesus pretiosus*
Snakehead, Striped *Channa striata*
Snapper, Red *Lutjanus blackfordi*
Spadefish, Atlantic *Chaetodipterus faber*
Squawfish, Colorado *Ptychocheilus lucius*
Squirrelfish (Soldierfish) *Holocentrus ascensionis*
Stargazer, Southern *Astroscopus y-graecum*
Stickleback, Brook *Eucalia inconstans*
Sting Ray, Southern *Dasyatis americana*
Sturgeon, Atlantic *Acipenser oxyrhynchus*
Surgeonfish *Acanthurus leucosternon*
Swallower, Black *Chiasmodon niger*
Swordfish *Xiphias gladius*
Swordtail, Mexican *Xiphophorus hellerii*
Tarpon *Tarpon atlanticus*
Tautog *Tautoga onitis*
Tilefish *Lopholatilus chamaeleonticeps*
Torpedo, Atlantic *Torpedo nobiliana*
Torpedo, Pacific *Torpedo californica*
Triggerfish, Common *Balistes carolinensis*
Triggerfish, Undulate *Balistapus undulatus*
Trout, Brook *Salvelinus fontinalis*
Trout, Brown *Salmo trutta*
Trout, Lake *Salvelinus namaycush*
Trout, Rainbow *Salmo gairdnerii*
Trunkfish, Blue *Ostracion lentiginosum*
Trunkfish, Common *Lactophrys trigonus*
Tuna, Bluefin *Thunnus thynnus*
Tuna, Yellowfin *Thunnus albacares*
Turbot, Diamond *Hypsopsetta guttulata*
Turbot, Spotted *Pleuronichthys ritteri*
Weakfish *Cynoscion regalis*
Whitebait (Tidewater Silverside) *Menidia beryllina*
Whiting, Walleye Pollack *Theragra chalco-grammus*
Wrasse, Birdfish *Gomphosus varius*
Wrasse, Cuckoo *Labrus ossifagus*
Wrasse, Lipfish *Labroides dimidiatus*
Wrasse, Rainbow *Labroides phthirophagus*

Bibliography

General Ichthyology

*Curtis, Brian, *The Life Story of the Fish*. Peter Smith, 1962.

Daniel, John Franklin, *The Elasmobranch Fishes* (2nd ed.). University of California Press, 1928.

Grassé, P. P., ed., *Traité de Zoologie* (Vol. XIII, *Agnathes et Poissons* 1958). Masson, Paris.

Harmer, S. F., and A. E. Shipley, eds., *The Cambridge Natural History* (Vol. VII, *Fishes*, 1910). Macmillan and Co., London.

Herald, Earl S., *Living Fishes of the World*. Doubleday, 1961.

Jordan, David Starr, *A Guide to the Study of Fishes* (2 vols.). Henry Holt, 1905.

Kyle, Harry M., *The Biology of Fishes*. Macmillan, 1926.

Lagler, Karl F., John E. Bardach and Robert R. Miller, *Ichthyology*. John Wiley & Sons, 1962.

Lanham, Url, *The Fishes*. Columbia University Press, 1962.

Norman, J. R., *A History of Fishes*. Hill & Wang, 1958.

Norman, J. R., and F. C. Fraser, *Field Book of Giant Fishes*. G. P. Putnam's Sons, 1949.

Vesey-Fitzgerald, Brian, and Francesca LaMonte, *Game Fish of the World*. Harper & Brothers, 1949.

*Zim, Herbert S., and Hurst H. Shoemaker, *Fishes*. Golden Press, 1956.

Anatomy and Physiology

Bertin, L., *Eels: A Biological Study*. Cleaver-Hume, London, 1956.

Brown, Margaret E., ed., *The Physiology of Fishes* (2 vols.). Academic Press, 1957.

*Colbert, Edwin H., *Evolution of the Vertebrates*. John Wiley & Sons, 1955.

†Goodrich, Edwin S., *Studies on the Structure and Development of Vertebrates* (2 vols.). Dover, 1958.

Gregory, William King, *Evolution Emerging* (2 vols.). Macmillan, 1951.

Kent, George C., Jr., *Comparative Anatomy of the Vertebrates*. McGraw-Hill, 1954.

Romer, Alfred S., *Vertebrate Paleontology* (2nd ed.). University of Chicago Press, 1945.

Walter, Herbert E., and Leonard P. Sayles, *Biology of the Vertebrates* (3rd ed.). Macmillan, 1959.

Weichert, Charles K., *Representative Chordates*. McGraw-Hill, 1959.

Yapp, W. B., *An Introduction to Animal Physiology*. Oxford University Press, London, 1960.

Young, J. Z., *The Life of Vertebrates* (2nd ed.). Oxford University Press, London, 1962.

Marine Fishes

Breder, Charles M., Jr., *Field Book of Marine Fishes of the Atlantic Coast* (rev. ed.). G. P. Putnam's Sons, 1948.

Coppleson, V. M., *Shark Attack*. Angus & Robertson, London, 1959.

Helm, Thomas, *Shark! Unpredictable Killer of the Sea*. Dodd, Mead, 1961.

LaMonte, Francesca, *Marine Game Fishes of the World*. Doubleday, 1952.

Perlmutter, Alfred, *Guide to Marine Fishes*. New York University Press, 1961.

U.S. Department of the Interior, *Fishes of the Gulf of Maine*. Government Printing Office, 1953.

Wells, A. Laurence, *The Observer's Book of Sea Fishes*. Frederick Warne, London, 1958.

Fresh-water Fishes

Hubbs, Carl L., and Karl F. Lagler, *Fishes of the Great Lakes Region* (rev. ed.). Cranbrook Institute of Science, 1958.

Schindler, Otto, *Guide to Freshwater Fishes*. Thames and Hudson, 1957.

Trautman, Milton B., *The Fishes of Ohio*. Ohio State University Press, 1957.

Wells, A. Laurence, *The Observer's Book of Freshwater Fishes*. Frederick Warne, London, 1961.

The Oceans

Carrington, Richard, *A Biography of the Sea*. Basic Books, 1960.

*Carson, Rachel L., *The Sea Around Us* (rev. ed.). Oxford University Press, 1961.

*Coker, R. E., *This Great and Wide Sea*. University of North Carolina Press, 1947.

Cowen, Robert C., *Frontiers of the Sea*. Doubleday, 1960.

Douglas, John Scott, *The Story of the Oceans*. Dodd, Mead, 1952.

Ommanney, F. D., *The Ocean* (2nd ed.). Oxford University Press, 1961.

Russell, Frederick Stratten, and Charles Maurice Yonge, *The Seas: Our Knowledge of Life in the Sea and How It Is Gained*. Frederick Warne, London, 1928.

Sverdrup, H.U., Martin W. Johnson and R.H. Fleming, *The Oceans: Their Physics, Chemistry and General Biology*. Prentice-Hall, 1942.

Fishing and Fisheries

†California Department of Fish and Game, *Results of Tagging Experiments in California Waters on the Sardine (Sardinops caerulea)*. State Printing Office, 1945.

†California Department of Fish and Game, *Tuna Marking, A Progress Report*. State Printing Office, 1953.

Farrington, S. Kip, Jr., *Fishing the Pacific*. Coward-McCann, 1953.

Migdalski, Edward C., *Angler's Guide to the Salt Water Game Fishes*. The Ronald Press, 1958.

†U.S. Department of the Interior, *Fishery Statistics of the United States, 1960*. Government Printing Office, 1962. †U.S. Department of the Interior, *Sonic Tracking of Adult Salmon at Bonneville Dam, 1957*. Government Printing Office, 1960.

Fish Raising

Axelrod, Herbert R., and William Vorderwinkler, *Encyclopedia of Tropical Fishes*. T.F.H. Publications, 1962.

Innes, William T., *Exotic Aquarium Fishes* (19th ed.). Innes Publishing, 1956.

Mann, Lucile Quarry, *Tropical Fish*. Sentinel Books, 1947.

McInerny, Derek, and Geoffrey Gerard, *All About Tropical Fish*. Macmillan, 1958.

Miscellaneous

*Bailey, R. M., et al., *A List of Common and Scientific Names of Fishes from the United States and Canada*. American Fisheries Society, 1960.

Beebe, William, *Half Mile Down*. Harcourt, Brace, 1934.

Buchsbaum, Ralph, and Mildred Buchsbaum, *Basic Ecology*. Boxwood Press, 1957.

Burton, Maurice, *Under the Sea*. Franklin Watts, 1960.

*Cousteau, Captain Jacques-Yves, with Frédéric Dumas, *The Silent World*. Harper & Brothers, 1953.

Davis, Charles C., *The Marine and Fresh-water Plankton*. Michigan State University Press, 1955.

Drimmer, Frederick, ed., *The Animal Kingdom* (3 vols.). Garden City Books, 1954.

Dugan, James, *Man under the Sea*. Harper & Brothers, 1956.

Halstead, Bruce W., *Dangerous Marine Animals*. Cornell Maritime Press, 1959.

Hardy, Alister C., *The Open Sea* (Vol. II, *Fish and Fisheries*, 1959). Houghton Mifflin.

Marshall, N. B., *Aspects of Deep Sea Biology*. Hutchinson, London, 1954.

Morton, J. E., *Molluscs*. Harper & Brothers, 1960.

Odum, Eugene P., *Fundamentals of Ecology*. W. B. Saunders, 1953.

Ray, Carleton, and Elgin Ciampi, *The Underwater Guide to Marine Life*. A. S. Barnes, 1956.

Roule, Louis, *Fishes, Their Journeys and Migrations*. W. W. Norton, 1933.

†Schmidt, Johannes, *Danish Eel Investigations During 25 Years, 1905-1930*. Carlsberg Foundation, Copenhagen, 1935.

Schultz, Leonard P., with Edith M. Stern, *The Ways of Fishes*. D. Van Nostrand, 1948.

* Also available in paperback edition.

† Only available in paperback edition.

Index

Picture Credits

Credits for pictures from left to right are separated by commas, top to bottom by dashes.

Cover: Don Ollis   8: Fritz Goro   10, 11, 12: Martha Alexander   13: Peg Estey—Martha Alexander   14, 15: Matt Greene   17: John H. Tashjian   18: E. S. Shinn   19: top right Ralph Royle from Photo Researchers, Inc.   20 through 23: Rudolf Freund   24: Douglas Faulkner   25: Stan Wayman from Rapho Guillumette—Douglas Faulkner   26, 27: Villaret from Rapho Guillumette—Douglas Faulkner (2), Dr. Carleton Ray-New York Aquarium   28: Stan Wayman from Rapho Guillumette   29: Lilo Hess   30, 31: Fritz Goro—Fred Baldwin from Lensgroup   32, 33: Dr. I. Eibl-Eibesfeldt   34: Andreas Feininger   36: Peg Estey   37: Matt Greene   38 through 43: Peg Estey   45: Douglas Faulkner   46, 47: Jack J. Kunz   48, 49: Robert F. Ames, Ernest L. Libby   50: John H. Tashjian, Constance P. Warner   51: Douglas Faulkner—Constance P. Warner—John H. Tashjian, Lilo Hess   52, 53: top Don Ollis; bottom Robert F. Ames, John H. Tashjian (3)   54: Ernest L. Libby—Douglas Faulkner   55: Douglas Faulkner—Gene Wolfsheimer   56: Marine Studios, Marineland, Florida—J. R. Eyerman   57: J. R. Eyerman   58: John H. Tashjian   60: Rene Martin   62, 63: Martha Alexander   64: Peg Estey   67: Douglas Faulkner courtesy Peabody Museum, Yale University   68, 69: Rene Martin   70: John Dominis   71: Lilo Hess   72: Harold E. Edgerton—Lilo Hess   73: Ernst Zollinger—Lilo Hess   74, 75: John G. Shedd Aquarium, Gene Wolfsheimer—Jean Marie Bauffle   76: Ernest L. Libby   78: Peg Estey   79 through 83: Martha Alexander   85: Jack Fields   86: Jack J. Kunz   87, 88, 89: Peter Gimbel   90: Russ Kinne from Photo Researchers, Inc.—Dr. Carleton Ray-New York Aquarium   91: Hans Hass—Ernest L. Libby   92: Coles Phinizy   93: Andreas Feininger—Douglas Faulkner courtesy Peabody Museum, Yale University   94, 95: Lennart Nilsson—Stan Wayman from Rapho Guillumette, Ernest L. Libby at Marine Studios, Marineland, Florida   96, 97: Ernest L. Libby at Marine Studios, Marineland, Florida—Elgin T. Ciampi at Florida's Silver Springs, Parker Studio at Gulfarium, Florida   98: Gene Wolfsheimer   100 through 103: Peg Estey   104: Martha Alexander—Peg Estey   105: Martha Alexander   107: Tom Reed   108, 109: Douglas Wilson   110: F. Ronald Hayes—Gene Wolfsheimer   111: F. Ronald Hayes—Tom Hutchins from Black Star   112, 113: Wallace Kirkland   114: Douglas Faulkner   115: Ken Libby   116: Gjon Mili   118, 119: Treat Davidson from National Audubon Society   120: Lennart Nilsson   124, 125: Peg Estey   126, 127: Rudolf Freund   131: Albert Querio   132 through 135: Elgin T. Ciampi at Florida's Silver Springs   136, 137: Ernest L. Libby, Ron Church—John G. New   138: Gene Wolfsheimer from Photo Researchers, Inc.   139: Walter A. Starck II—Douglas Wilson, Don Ollis—Laverne Pederson   140, 141: H. Kacher except top left Ron Church; right center Douglas Faulkner   142: Douglas Faulkner   143: Lennart Nilsson—Fritz Goro   144, 145: George Skadding   146, 147: N. R. Farbman   148: Elgin T. Ciampi   150, 151: Rene Martin   154: Matt Greene   155: Martha Alexander   159: Don LeBlanc from Annan Photo Service   160, 161: Rolf Klep   162: Dr. T. G. Northcote, Ronald Thompson from Annan Photo Service—Fritz Goro   163: Otto Hagel   164, 165: E. S. Shinn, Logan O. Smith, Fritz Goro—Hans Hass   166, 167: Elgin T. Ciampi   168: Lennart Nilsson from Black Star   170 through 175: Matt Greene   179: Larry Burrows   180, 181: Eliot Elisofon   182, 183: top right U.S. Bureau of Commercial Fisheries—bottom Leonard McCombe   184: Davis Pratt from Rapho Guillumette   185: Otto Hagel   Back Cover: Matt Greene

Acknowledgments

The editors are particularly indebted to Carl L. Hubbs, Professor of Biology Emeritus, Scripps Institution of Oceanography, University of California, San Diego, who read and criticized the entire book, and to Robert L. Edwards, Assistant Director for Fisheries Programs, U.S. Bureau of Commercial Fisheries, Washington, D.C., Bobb Shaeffer, Curator, and Marlyn Mangus, Scientific Assistant, Department of Vertebrate Paleontology, The American Museum of Natural History, who also read the book and criticized chapters in their fields. The editors are also indebted to Stewart Springer, U.S. Fish and Wildlife Service; James W. Atz, Associate Curator, Department of Ichthyology, The American Museum of Natural History; Harold F. Roellig; Daniel Merriman, Associate Professor of Biology, Yale University; John H. Ostrom, Assistant Curator, Vertebrate Paleontology, Peabody Museum, Yale; H. S. Gallager; John E. Bardach, Professor of Fisheries and Zoology, University of Michigan; Phyllis H. Cahn, Associate Professor of Biology, Stern College for Women, Yeshiva University; Dr. Perry W. Gilbert, Director, Mote Marine Laboratory, Sarasota, Florida; Dr. John E. Randall, Bernice P. Bishop Museum, Honolulu, Hawaii; and Gerald R. Allen, Eniwetok Marine Biological Laboratory, Eniwetok, Marshall Islands.